PRAYING GOD'S WILL *for* YOUR LIFE

student edition

STORMIE OMARTIAN

TRANSIT®

A JANET THOMA BOOK

THOMAS NELSON PUBLISHERS®
Nashville

A Division of Thomas Nelson, Inc.
www.ThomasNelson.com

Published in Nashville, Tennessee, by Thomas Nelson, Inc.

Unless otherwise noted, Scripture quotations are from THE NEW KING JAMES VERSION. Copyright © 1979, 1980, 1982, Thomas Nelson, Inc. Publishers.

Scripture quotations noted NIV are from the HOLY BIBLE: NEW INTERNATIONAL VERSION ®. Copyright © 1973, 1978, 1984 by International Bible Society. Used by permission of Zondervan Publishing House. All rights reserved.

Scripture quotations noted NLT are from the *Holy Bible*, New Living Translation, copyright © 1996. Used by permission of Tyndale House Publishers, Inc., Wheaton, Illinois 60189. All rights reserved.

Scripture quotations noted NCV are from *The Holy Bible, New Century Version*, copyright © 1987, 1988, 1991 by W Publishing Group, a division of Thomas Nelson, Inc. Used by permission.

Some of this book's content was previously published as *Finding Peace for Your Heart*.

Library of Congress Cataloging-in-Publication Data

Omartian, Stormie.
    Praying God's will for your life / Stormie Omartian.— Student Ed.
      p. cm.
    Includes bibliographical references.
    ISBN 0-7852-6114-1 (pbk.)
    1. Christian women—Religious life. 2. God—Will—Meditations.
3. Prayer—Christianity. 4. Devotional calendars. I. Title.
    BV4527.O45 2004
    248.4—dc22

Printed in the United States of America
04 05 06 07 08 PHX 6 5 4 3 2

CONTENTS

Part One

HOW CAN I KNOW GOD?

Establishing an Intimate Relationship

Chapter One

DOES GOD HAVE A
PLAN FOR MY LIFE?

"YOU'RE WORTHLESS, AND YOU'LL NEVER AMOUNT TO anything," my mother said as she pushed me into the little closet underneath the stairway and slammed the door. "Now stay in there until I can stand to see your face!" The sound of her footsteps faded as she walked down the small hallway back to the kitchen.

I wasn't really sure what I had done to warrant being locked in the closet again, but I knew it must be bad. I knew *I* must be bad, and I believed that all the negative things she had ever said about me were surely accurate—after all, she was my mother.

The closet was a small, rectangular storage area underneath the stairs where the dirty laundry was kept in an old wicker basket. I sat on top of the pile of clothes and pulled my feet in tight to eliminate the possibility of being touched by the mice that periodically streaked across the floor.

I felt lonely, unloved, and painfully afraid as I waited in that

3

dark hole for the seemingly endless amount of time it took for her to remember I was there or for my father to return. Either event would mean my release from the closet and from the devastatingly closed-in feeling of being buried alive and forgotten.

As you can probably tell from just this one incident, I was raised by a mentally ill mother, and, among other atrocities, I spent much of my early childhood locked in a closet. Although certain people were aware of her bizarre behavior from time to time, her mental illness wasn't clearly identified until I was in my late teens. During all my growing-up years, my mother's extremely erratic behavior left me with feelings of hopelessness, helplessness, and deep emotional pain.

A SENSE OF DREAD

As far back as I can remember, I woke up every morning with an overwhelming sense of dread. It's the same feeling you have when you wake up for the first time after someone you love has tragically and suddenly died. The reality of it comes flooding back to you, and you realize it wasn't a bad dream after all. You wish with all of your being that it was not true, but it is and you have to face it. The thought of getting through the day brings such a weight of depression it requires a major effort to even get out of bed.

That's exactly the way I always felt, even though no one had died. No one, that is, except me. I was dying on a daily basis. I could feel it, but I didn't know what to do about it.

No one ever saw my struggle, so I pretended everything was fine. And I got very good at it when I became an adult.

I stayed as busy as possible, with as many people as possible, in order to create a diversion so grand that I didn't have to feel the terrible purposelessness of my life. But there was always that moment of extreme aloneness, with no noise and no activity, when I crossed over from sleep to consciousness. In those first waking moments, the deafening quiet exposed the futility of my life and it was unbearable.

I often thought of suicide as a means of escape because I didn't want to wake up again with that dreaded feeling and have to face another day. I certainly couldn't imagine that things could ever be any different from the way they were. I had spent a lifetime trying to transform myself and to change my circumstances, and I found I was completely powerless to do so. The way I was and the way my life was going had been entirely unacceptable to me for far too long. And I could see no other way out.

Of course I had been on an extensive search to find meaning for my life. But the god I was pursuing in my occult practices was a weak and distant god who really couldn't do anything for me unless I could be good enough, or enlightened enough, or religious enough, or smart enough to somehow get to him and prove I was worthy. I was fairly certain he had more important things to do than help me.

Realizing that I was without a god or anyone else to come to my aid, I decided it was all up to me. I was in charge of my destiny. I had to make myself acceptable to others. I had to make my life the way it should be. The problem was, I knew I couldn't do it.

I had been a singer and an actress on television for about eight years, and I was finding it increasingly difficult to hide behind either of those occupations for any length of time. The emptiness inside of me was growing at an alarming rate, and I felt so fragile that I knew it wouldn't take much for me to crack like an eggshell.

UNUSUAL RECORDING SESSIONS

One week I was asked to sing on a series of recording sessions for a Christian musical. I was glad to have the work, and making records was far easier than the labor-intensive schedule of a television show. Back in those days we did TV shows live, so the rehearsal schedule was intense. You had to have the dance routine, dialogue, and songs you were singing down so perfectly that you wouldn't make a mistake when the cameras were rolling and you were seen live in front of millions of people.

When I arrived at the recording studio for the first session, it was filled with people, most of whom I had never met. There was a sense of peace and calm, and everyone was friendly, warm, and welcoming—quite different from what I was used to in television. My spirits began to lift immediately. This was amazing because it was an early-morning session, which means I had not had much time to work out of my traditional early-morning depression.

During the first break of the day I met more of the singers, musicians, and recording crew. They all had certain common qualities about them that I found very appealing: a sense of simplicity, fullness, and purpose. Someone might question how I could identify a sense of fullness, and I don't know how to explain it, except to say that it stood in stark contrast to my own emptiness. I could also sense that they were not into drugs, alcohol, and promiscuity. Again, there was that contrast.

My friend Terry was the contractor on this session, which meant she was in charge of hiring all of the singers. She was one of the best studio singers in Los Angeles, and I had worked with her often. She always sang the lead and I would stand next to her and sing second. I think she liked working with me because I never tried to compete with her. Instead, I recognized her expertise and tried to blend as well as I could with what she did. At this session she took me under her wing because she was aware that I didn't know many people there.

We were all singing three to a microphone. On our microphone, Terry was in the middle and another girl and I were on either side of her, looking off the same metal music stand. After that first break was over and we were recording again, I reached up to adjust my headphones. When I brought my hand down, the gold ring on my hand hit the metal music stand and made a loud bang. That brought the session to an immediate halt.

This was back in the days when there were none of the techno-logical tricks studios have today. A mistake of this magnitude meant we had to start that whole section of music all over again, which was not good because it had been perfect up to that point. Normally something like this could have been enough to keep me from getting called to work again. It wasn't just that I had made a mistake; it was the money it cost the producers for the time involved in having to record it all over again.

I felt badly about what happened and apologized profusely. I expected to receive angry glares, a severe shunning at lunch break, and a call asking me not to come back for the rest of the sessions. Instead, everyone acted like it was no big deal and as if they still valued me as a person. The only thing that happened was that the conductor politely said if anyone else was wearing rings or bracelets we should remove them, which we all did. I felt like crying at that point, not just because of making the mistake, but because of the love and mercy I had been shown. It was not the norm in my experience.

It was on our lunch break, when we went out together in a large group, that I learned that everyone on the session was a Christian except me. They all talked about their futures, some of which I gathered were even more precarious than mine. Yet none of them feared the future as I did. I feared I didn't have one. They knew they had one because they understood God had a plan for their lives. They said that as long as they walked in the will of God, their future was secure in His hands. I had never heard of such a thing.

Obviously their God was different from the gods I had been pursuing. He was personal. He was warm. He had a plan for each person's life. I didn't say anything about my situation because I did not want to expose that I wasn't a Christian and possibly embarrass Terry. She already knew that I was not a believer, but I didn't think that the others did. Now, looking back, I'm sure they all knew. They were probably as much aware of my emptiness as I was of their fullness.

Each day of the sessions I found myself increasingly attracted to the sense of purpose these people had about their lives. I wanted that so badly, but I didn't know how I could even get close to it. I was sure that a person must have to be born under a different star than I was in order to attain it. Yet I couldn't get the idea of God's will out of my mind.

I wonder if God has a plan for my life? I thought to myself. That would mean I didn't have to make life happen. *But what if His plan for me is to be a missionary in Siberia? Death would be better. How do I find out what God's plan is for me?*

I thought about this for the next few days of the sessions. I tried to learn more from each of the singers at every lunch break without letting them know why I was interested. I didn't want anyone pressuring me to have a life of purpose. Besides, being miserable was familiar to me, and I was more comfortable with what I knew.

After the last session on the final day, as I was in my car on the way home, I prayed to this God of theirs without knowing if He could even hear me. "God, if You have a will for my life," I said, "I need to know what it is and what to do about it."

I heard no reply. As I suspected, this God would probably never listen to someone like me. I went on with my life as it was, spiraling downward at an ever-increasing pace.

Over the course of the next few months many things happened to me, one of which changed my life forever: I met the God that Terry and her friends had been talking about. The simple prayer I had prayed in the car, to a God I didn't even know, was answered.

BASIC STEPS TO FULFILL GOD'S PLAN

That happened years ago, and today I know that the will of God is not some mysterious thing that only a few select people can understand. It's there for each one of us, if we take the necessary steps to find it. The steps are simple, but often for that very reason we don't bother to take them. Yet we *have* to take them because we can never be happy until we understand God's will for our lives and are living in it.

From that time on, I continually prayed, "God, tell me what to do. Show me what steps to take. Guide me where I need to go." And God always answered those prayers. He spoke to my heart saying, "Just be in My presence. I'll make things happen the way they are supposed to."

In the following months and years I learned that life could be much simpler than I ever dreamed. Knowing that God has a plan for you simplifies everything because you don't have to figure it all out and make it all happen. You just have to look to the Lord, knowing that He has it all figured out and He will make it happen.

It didn't matter what my situation was at the moment; all I had to do was take the next step the Lord was showing me. As I did, I began to see a solid way of living, which I could explain to other people. I could say, "You just take these steps. As long as you are walking with God and living His way, you are not likely to get off the path. And if by chance you do, He will get you right back on. That's because you've been listening to God's voice, and you will feel in your heart when you violate one of His directions."

The following chapters in this book present the questions you may have regarding these basic steps to establish an intimate relationship with God, to lay a solid foundation in His truth, and to learn to walk in His ways. All of these things are the will of God for your life, as revealed in His Word.

At the end of each chapter are short prayers. As you read this book I suggest that you see what a difference prayer can make in your life. Try praying for five or ten minutes every day as you consider each of these twenty questions.

Now let me tell you about each of these steps and how I learned of their importance in our lives.

Chapter Two

DOES GOD CARE
ABOUT ME?

I TOOK THE HANDFUL OF SLEEPING PILLS A FRIEND HAD just given me and added them to my growing collection in a little gold box in the back of the bottom drawer of my bedroom dresser. *I have nearly enough to do the job right this time,* I told myself. Deliberately and methodically I planned my suicide. I wanted to make it look like an accidental overdose so my sister and dad wouldn't bear any guilt.

I had tried to kill myself when I was fourteen by downing an odd combination of drugs in our bathroom, but they only succeeded in making me very sick. Since that failed attempt, I had thrown myself into everything I could possibly find to get out of my dark, emotional prison cell. Unfortunately, every so-called "key to life" I tried only led me closer to death and further from the freedom, peace, and release I so desperately sought.

Since then I'd had plenty of good psychiatric and psychological counseling, especially if measured in terms of how much money I had paid, and I was grateful for each doctor as he kept me from destroying myself. Yet at twenty-eight years old, fourteen years after my suicide attempt, I still felt as if I were down in a dark hole, and I couldn't produce the strength to pick myself up one more time. Death was again the only solution I could see. I was amazed that in all those years of struggle my life had still come to nothing.

At that low point, which was a few months after the series of recording sessions, my friend Terry said, "I can see you're not doing well, Stormie. Won't you come with me and talk to my pastor?" Sensing my reluctance, she quickly added, "You've got nothing to lose."

I silently bore witness to her accurate assessment of my situation and agreed to go even though I wanted nothing whatsoever to do with any kind of religion. My experience with churches had been that they made me feel more dead than I did already.

Terry took me to meet Pastor Jack Hayford from the nearby Church on the Way, and it turned out to be like no other meeting I'd ever had. We met him at a restaurant for lunch, and from the moment he started talking, he had my full attention. He asked me a little about myself, but I was not open to revealing anything of my desperate circumstances. Even at this late hour in my life, I wanted to appear successful.

AN EVENTFUL MEETING

For more than an hour, Pastor Jack talked about God the way someone talks about a best friend. He said that at my invitation, God would come to live within me and transform my life from the inside out.

"If you receive Jesus, the relationship you can have with God will be so personal that every part of your being can be shared with Him and His with you," Pastor Jack explained. "You would never be without hope or purpose again."

I had no trouble listening to him talk about God because I knew there was a spirit realm. I had seen enough supernatural manifestations through my delving into the occult to convince me of their reality. But when he started talking about receiving Jesus and being born again, I winced.

> If God is for us, who can be against us?
>
> ROMANS 8:31

I had frequently seen people standing on street corners, waving black books and screaming, "Jesus saves!" and "You're all going to hell!" to everyone passing by. Because of them, I feared that accepting Jesus meant having an intellectual lobotomy, which would turn me into an unthinking, self-righteous, coldhearted, beat-people-over-the-head-with-your-Bible kind of person with whom the reality of other people's true pain never registered. I had noticed, however, that neither Pastor Jack nor Terry was anything like that.

Fortunately, Pastor Jack saw through my fears and didn't push me for any commitment. Instead he sent me home with three books: the first, about the life of Jesus, was the gospel of John in book form; the second one, *The Screwtape Letters* by C. S. Lewis, was about the reality of evil; and the third was a book about the working of the Holy Spirit of God in people's lives.

"Let's talk again next week in my office and you can let me know then what you think of these books," Pastor Jack said as we ended our meeting. We agreed, and I went home to start reading. Something about what Terry and Pastor Jack said and did that day made me want to find out what they knew that I didn't.

As I read the pages of each book, I realized that for years I had believed lies about Jesus, judging Him from what I'd heard of Him without really knowing Him. His name and reputation had been so maligned, mocked, misinterpreted, joked and lied about for so long that I dismissed Him from any possible connection with my life. As I read I also realized that God was not the cold and distant force I had thought, but rather a loving and powerful Father who sent us a means of total restoration through Jesus, His Son.

The more I read, the more I saw that my New Age belief that there is no evil in the world except what exists in people's minds was a deception. As C. S. Lewis's book dramatized the activity of Satan, the source of the horrible things that happen to people became obvious. There is an evil force intent on our destruction, and Satan, the head of that force, is real and very much our enemy.

As I seriously pondered all I read, I also thought about Terry and Pastor Jack and how much I admired them. They were not phony, stupid, or unloving. They had an inherent, simple beauty and a bold confidence that radiated God's power because they had acknowledged Him as Lord of their lives.

THE MOST IMPORTANT STEP YOU'LL EVER TAKE

One of the main reasons people are lonely and distressed is that they have not acknowledged God as Savior, as Father, as Holy Spirit, as Lord in every area of life, and as the Name who answers every need. Until we have aligned ourselves properly with God, nothing in life will fall into place as it should.

GOD'S WAY IS LIFE—NOT DEATH

Christian singer Rebecca St. James, a young woman who earned a Grammy nomination for the "Best Rock Gospel Album" at the age of nineteen, has a question-and-answer time as part of her concerts. During that time young people can ask about things that are on their minds. At one concert in California, a young person asked her, "What do you think of Kurt Cobain's suicide?"

At first Rebecca didn't know what to say, so she prayed that God would give her the right words.

Then she said that Kurt Cobain (lead singer/songwriter for the punk rock group Nirvana, who shot himself in April 1994) was an example of someone who absolutely lived for self. "His death was the ultimate end to his own selfishness." She went on to say, "When we decide to live for ourselves rather than choosing to live God's way, that's exactly what we do—condemn ourselves to destruction. To some extent, selfishness always leads to death of some sort. If you allow selfishness to have its way, you are really letting yourself slowly die inside. God's way is life—not death."[1]

As I read the books Pastor Jack gave me, I realized this was what I had always been looking for. God loved and cared about me and my circumstances. If I acknowledged His presence in my life, He would transform me. I looked forward to my next meeting with Pastor Jack and Terry.

If you have never acknowledged God's presence in your life, you might want to do so now by praying the first prayer below. If you have done so in the past, you may want to renew your commitment to God by praying the second prayer. Or you can use these prayers as a guide and speak to God as if He was sitting across the table from you.

Prayers

To Acknowledge God's Presence

Lord, I have not recognized You as the God of the universe. Forgive me for that mistake. I know You care about me. Help me sense Your presence so strongly in my life that I never doubt it.

To Renew Your Awareness of God's Presence

Lord, I know You are God of the universe, and I recognize that you are present in my life. Please help me sense Your hand on me as I go about my daily tasks. I love You, Lord, and I thank You for Your love and care for me.

Chapter Three

IS JESUS MY SAVIOR?

AS I READ THE BOOKS PASTOR JACK GAVE ME, I COULD immediately see two reasons to acknowledge Jesus as my Savior. *The first reason was to be completely free of guilt.*

My sense of guilt was overwhelming, but for all the wrong reasons. I had no remorse for things I had done that were wrong. I saw actions like lying and love affairs as means of survival and refused to allow myself to feel bad about them. Whenever I did feel guilty, I assumed it was because my mother had instilled it in me with her constant anger. She had a way of making everything I did seem evil; some days I even felt guilty for being alive.

Everyone has some kind of guilt for mistakes of the past. Sometimes it's for things we know we've done; sometimes it's deep regret over what we fear we could have prevented; and sometimes it's for violation of certain natural laws we're not even aware of violating. Whatever the reason, the load of guilt sits on us with crushing weight, and unless it's eliminated it separates us from the fullness of life.

How do you and I live with painful regrets? *If only I'd . . . ; If I just hadn't . . .; If only I hadn't cheated on that test;* or *If I hadn't gone to that party where I knew there would be alcohol, I wouldn't have been so tempted to drink.* These thoughts echo the agony of situations that are over and done. And there's no way to live with the truth of it unless you push it down deep and never allow yourself to feel it again.

Or how do you and I live with our guilty feelings over things that aren't our fault, but we fear might be? *If I'd been more obedient, maybe my dad wouldn't have left us. If I hadn't fought with my mother, maybe she wouldn't have gotten so sick.*

Guilt upon guilt piles up to become a burden that is literally unbearable.

Finally, what about our guilt over things we've done that violated God's laws, laws of which we weren't even aware at the time? No matter how much a girl or woman who has had an abortion believes her decision was right, I've never heard one say, "I've been fulfilled and enriched by this experience." She may feel relieved of a burden, but she never thinks, *What a wonderful thing I've done. I know I have truly realized God's purpose for my life and I am a better person because of it.* Whether she acknowledges it or not, the guilt is there because she has violated a law of nature.

What or who can take this guilt away? A friend's saying, "Don't worry about it . . . It wasn't your fault . . . You can't blame yourself," never gets rid of what you feel inside. Only God's forgiveness can do that.

When we receive Jesus, we are immediately released from the penalty for our past mistakes. For the first time in my life I felt free from having to face the failure of my past on a moment-to-moment basis.

The second important reason to receive Jesus was to have the peace of knowing that my future was secure. And not only is my eternal future secure—Jesus said anyone who believes in Him will have everlasting life (John 6:40)—but my future in this life is also secure. God promises that if we acknowledge Him, He will guide us safely where we need to go (Prov. 3:6). This doesn't mean that we will instantly have all of our problems solved and never again know pain, but we will have the power within us to reach our full potential. We can never find any greater security than that.

LIFE BEFORE DEATH

You may have been born into a Christian family or have attended a Christian church all your life, but if you haven't told God that you want to receive Jesus, you haven't been born into the kingdom of God. You can't inherit it, get it by osmosis, transplant it, implant it—or wish upon a star for it. You have to declare your faith before the Lord.

BEING BORN AGAIN

One night Nicodemus came to Jesus and said, "Teacher, we know you are a teacher sent from God, because no one can do the miracles you do unless God is with him."

Jesus answered, "I tell you the truth, unless one is born again, he cannot be in God's kingdom."

Nicodemus said, "But if a person is already old, how can he be born again? He cannot enter his mother's body again. So how can a person be born a second time?"

But Jesus answered, "I tell you the truth, unless one is born from water and the Spirit, he cannot enter God's kingdom. Human life comes from human parents, but spiritual life comes from the Spirit" (John 3:2–6 NCV).

Two teenage girls who were killed at Columbine High School when two teenage boys, Eric Harris and Dylan Klebold, turned their guns on fellow students, made this decision to accept Christ as Savior. One of those teenage girls was Cassie Bernall. The girl who died that day in April of 1999 was very different from the daughter her parents had known three years earlier. Her mother tells about Cassie's life in the book *She Said Yes*.

On December 20, 1996 Cassie's mother, Misty, remembered that her brother had given Cassie a "teen" Bible, which had a sort of study guide to give young readers some insights into dealing with their parents. Misty decided to look at the Bible to see if she could get some insights into improving her relationship with Cassie.

When Misty looked for the Bible in her daughter's room, she found a stack of unbelievable letters. Many of these letters were decorated with monkeys with vampire teeth, axes, knives, or mushrooms (for mind-altering drugs). One letter from Cassie's friend Mona talked about a teacher at the high school who had told Mona's parents about an F she had received. "Want to help me murder her?" Mona asked in the letter.

Another letter from Mona said, "I believe I am a vampire. We are everywhere," she said. "If you kill one of us, we will get you."

One letter from a friend advised Cassie, "Kill your parents! Murder is the answer to all of your problems. Make those scumbags pay for your suffering. Love you, me."[1]

Misty Bernall was both hurt and frightened. She and her husband, Brad, confronted Cassie when she came home from school. At first she said, "Oh, we didn't mean anything bad. . . ." Then when she realized that her parents would not accept this, she began screaming about how her parents had trampled on her rights by going through her bedroom. Cassie threatened to run away and kill herself.

The Bernalls knew they had to take immediate steps to protect

Cassie from the friends she was associating with. They filed a restraining order that kept Mona from contacting Cassie. They went to the youth pastor at their church, Bowles Community Church, and sought his advice. The only place Cassie was allowed to go in the next weeks and months was to youth group events.

They also switched her to a private Christian school. At first this proved disastrous. Cassie felt that the kids there hated her. Then she met Jamie, a fellow freshman. One day in the spring of 1997, Jamie invited Cassie to a youth retreat.

At this retreat, Cassie turned her life around. She told her mother that the date March 8, 1997, was a sort of second birthday—the day she was "reborn."

Her friend Jamie described what happened at that retreat to Cassie's parents six weeks after her death.

THE NIGHT THAT CHANGED CASSIE'S LIFE

There was a nighttime praise-and-worship service. I don't remember what the guy talked about, though the theme of the weekend was overcoming the temptations of evil and breaking out of the selfish life. It was the singing that for some reason just broke down Cassie's walls. . . . When she totally broke down, I was pretty shocked.

Actually we were outside the building, and Cassie was crying. She was pouring out her heart—I think she was praying—and asking God for forgiveness. Inside a lot of kids had been bringing things up to the altar—drug paraphernalia and stuff like that; they were breaking off their old bonds.

Cassie didn't have anything to bring up to the altar, but she was pouring out all these things she felt bad about and wanting to give them all up. . . .

After the service Cassie and I, and this guy named Kevin, and

> Justin, and Erin drove for like a quarter of a mile up the road and got out and stood under the stars up in the mountains there. We just stood there in silence for several minutes, totally in awe of God. It was phenomenal: our smallness, and the bigness of the sky. The bigness of God was so real.
>
> Later I noticed that Cassie's whole face had changed.[2]

Did this experience change Cassie's life? Her parents also noticed a change in her: she smiled as she hadn't for years and she began to treat her parents and her brother with genuine respect and affection.

Between her freshman and her sophomore years, Cassie asked to transfer from the private Christian school to Columbine High School. She said, "Mom, I can't witness to the kids at Christian school. I could reach out to many more people if I were in a public one."[3]

That's when her faith was tested for the last time. Josh, a sophomore, was in the library that day when Eric and Dylan attacked the students. He told Cassie's parents what he heard as he crouched under a desk.

THE COLUMBINE TRAGEDY

I couldn't see anything when those guys came up to Cassie, but I could recognize her voice. I could hear everything like it was right next to me. One of them asked her if she believed in God. She paused, like she didn't know what she was going to answer, and then she said yes. She must have been scared, but her voice didn't sound shaky. It was strong. Then they asked her why, though they didn't give her a chance to respond. They just blew her away.[4]

Another student who died on April 20, 1999 was Rachel Scott. Later, when her parents received the backpack she was wearing that day—a backpack that had been torn by the bullet that went through her body—they found her journal, which also bore the marks of that bullet. During the next weeks her parents went through this journal and read of her spiritual journey, which began when she accepted Christ as Savior during a church service in 1993. Rachel described it this way,

> Everyone was at the altar, and I felt so drawn to it. You have to understand that I was so young, and so for a twelve-year-old to be drawn that way, it was nothing short of God. I slowly walked up, till finally I reached the front. I sorta looked around and then closed my eyes and extended my hands toward heaven. I don't remember what I said, but I will never forget the feeling I had. That night, I accepted Jesus into my heart. I was saved.[5]

In the weeks after that Rachel's parents noticed a change in her. That change is recorded in her journal, which I will quote from in several chapters in this book. Rachel had great insight into her spiritual journey. She even predicted her death in an entry dated May 2, 1998: "This will be my last year, Lord. I have gotten what I can. Thank you."[6] In the six years between her acceptance of Christ as savior in 1993 and her death in 1999, Rachel lived this commitment at school and at home. Rachel Scott and Cassie Bernall live in heaven with Jesus today because of their faith.

When Jesus died on the cross, He also rose from the dead to break the power of death over anyone who receives His life. Jesus conquered death—whether at the end of our lives or in the multiple ways that we face death daily. In the death of our dreams, finances, health, or relationships, Jesus can bring His life to resurrect those dead places. Therefore we don't have to feel hopeless. He is the only one who can give us life before death as well as life hereafter. Without Him we die a little every day. With Him we become more and more alive.

THE DAY THAT CHANGED MY LIFE

When Terry and I met with Pastor Jack the week following our first meeting, he asked me directly, "Well, what did you think of the books I gave you?"

"I think they are the truth," I responded with uncharacteristic confidence.

"So would you like to receive God's life in you?" he asked openly.

"Yes," I said without hesitation. "I want that, and I want all that God has for me."

That day in October of 1970, I decided to believe Jesus was who He said He was and receive Him into my life.

After I prayed that prayer with Pastor Jack, Terry and I were leaving the office when he caught the arm of a young man walking by.

"Stormie, I want you to meet Paul, my assistant pastor," he said. "Tell him what just happened."

I was uneasy as I shook Paul's hand and said sheepishly, "I just received Jesus."

I half expected him to laugh and say, "You've got to be kidding!" Much to my amazement he said with a reassuring combination of sincerity and seriousness, "Praise God! That's wonderful." I smiled in response and it felt good.

There is release in telling someone you have received Jesus. It doesn't matter who. All that matters is that you have acknowledged Jesus to someone else so that it is firmly established. Even if you've known the Lord for a long time, it's good to do that frequently. Your belief in Him needs to be reconfirmed periodically.

It's also good to write the date you received the Lord in your Bible or in your diary or journal, just as Rachel did. This records your new birth date so that if you ever have doubt or confusion about whether it really happened, you will have it written in black and white. One of my friends was "born again" six or seven times because her emotions were fragile and her mind so clouded with oppression that she was never sure she had done it well enough the first time. That isn't necessary.

You are never born again by chance. When you receive Jesus, it is because God the Father is drawing you in. Jesus said, "No one can come to Me unless the Father who sent Me draws him" (John 6:44). Once God draws you in, it's done—once and for all. You are released from guilt, your future is secure, and you are saved from death in every part of your life.

THE TESTIMONY OF THOSE WHO HAVE GONE BEFORE

You may wonder, But how do I know that Jesus is really who He says He is? Here are two testimonies of men who lived during the time Christ was on earth:

John, a disciple of Christ, walked with Jesus during his three-year ministry. This apostle wrote the book of John in the Bible and also letters to some of the early churches. John told people in the first century:

"And we have seen and testify that the Father has sent the Son as Savior of the world. Whoever confesses that Jesus is the Son of God, God abides in him, and he in God" (1 John 4:14–15).

Paul, a devout Jew, persecuted the early Christians. On the road to Damascus he had an encounter with Christ when Jesus asked him, "Saul, Saul, why do you persecute me?" After this dramatic experience Saul became a Christian, and his name was changed to Paul. He said this about Jesus:

> "Therefore God also has highly exalted Him and given Him the name which is above every name, that at the name of Jesus every knee should bow, of those in heaven, and of those on earth, and of those under the earth, and that every tongue should confess that Jesus Christ is Lord, to the glory of God the Father" (Phil. 2:9–11).

THEN PASS IT ON

After I became a Christian, I began to talk to my friends about my experience, particularly my best friend, Diane. We had always been so close, and now we could not share the most important experience in my life. We had been into the occult together, and she thought I was crazy to get involved in this "Jesus thing." One day, however, she called me and was very depressed.

"The Lord would really make a difference in your life," I told her. "Jesus isn't like the gods we studied in the occult. Those gods don't have the power to set us free. Jesus does. He can set you free from your depression."

Apparently I convinced her of the major difference the Lord had made in my life, because she asked me to pray with her to receive Jesus as her Savior. It was the first time I had ever led anyone to the Lord, and I was nervous about whether I was doing it right. But I had heard Pastor Jack lead people to the Lord in his touching way, and so I remembered some of the things he said. The prayer at the end of this chapter is similar to the one I asked her to pray. If you want to receive Jesus into your life, you can pray this same prayer also.

Rachel Scott felt this same desire to influence her classmates. She wrote in her diary: "I want heads to turn in the halls when I walk by. I want them to stare at me, watching and wanting the light you have put in me. I want you to overflow my cup with your Spirit. . . . I want you to use me to reach the unreached."[7]

In another journal entry on April 20, 1998, Rachel wrote, "I am not going to apologize for speaking the Name of Jesus, I am not going to justify my faith to them, and I am not going to hide the light that God has put into me. If I have to sacrifice everything . . . I will."[8]

And the students did feel God's love from her, although Rachel probably did not know it. After her death her parents received e-mails from young people on their Web site. One of these was from a girl named Amber Jackson.

At a big school like Columbine, which has more than sixteen hundred students, many new students feel lonely. Amber certainly did. On her first day at school, she sat down in the corner of the cafeteria all by herself. But not for long.

Rachel walked up to her with a big smile on her face and said, "Hi, I'm Rachel Scott. Are you new at school?"

When Amber said yes, Rachel asked a bunch of her friends to have lunch with Amber. Rachel's kindness turned what could have been one of the worst days in Amber's life into one of the best days.

Before the shootings Amber moved to Georgia, and when she heard about the Columbine tragedy, she said that all she could think about was the young girl who had made such an impact on her life with such a simple but profound act of kindness. Amber also mentioned that in the time she was at Columbine she noticed Rachel greeting other new students in the same way.

How about you? Are you willing to accept Christ as Savior? Are you willing to pass this blessing on?

Prayers

To Receive Jesus as Savior

Jesus, I acknowledge You this day. I believe You are the Son of God as You say You are. Although it's hard to comprehend love so great, I believe You laid down your life for me so that I might have life eternally and abundantly now. I ask You to forgive me for not living Your way. I need You to help me become all You created me to be. Come into my life and fill me with Your Holy Spirit. Let all the death in me be crowded out by the power of Your presence, and this day turn my life into a new beginning.

If you don't feel comfortable with this prayer, then talk to Jesus as you would to a good friend, and confess you've made some mistakes. Tell Him you can't live without Him. Ask Him to forgive you and to come into your heart. Tell Him you receive Him as Lord, and thank Him for His eternal life and forgiveness.

If you wish to renew your commitment to Your Savior, pray the following prayer:

To Renew Your Commitment to Jesus as Your Savior

Jesus, I acknowledge Your presence in my life. I know that You live in me because I have accepted You as Savior. I know that You died for me and You are able to raise up the dead areas of my life. Show me where I am not walking fully in all You have for me. I make a new commitment to living Your way.

Chapter Four

IS GOD MY
HEAVENLY FATHER?

IT'S ONE THING TO KNOW JESUS; IT'S ANOTHER TO KNOW the Father. Salvation's purpose is not only to get us to Christ, but also to get us to the Father, where we understand our relationship with our Creator. Yet acknowledging God as your heavenly Father is sometimes difficult for people, especially if they didn't have a father or have been mistreated by a male parent or authority figure.

One young woman told me, "Don't talk to me about God being a father. My father forced me to have sex with him until I left home, and now I'm unable to have a normal relationship with any man at all." Another confided to me, "My father beat me every time he came home drunk, and now I hate him. How can I think of God as a father?" A middle-aged man said, "My father never did anything for me. He was a weakling. He contributed nothing to my life and then eventually deserted us. Don't mention the word *father*."

I never had a dad who abused me, and for that I am very grateful. Yet my dad never rescued me from my abusive mother, and he was the only one with the power and authority to do so. Because of that experience, I subconsciously felt God would not help me either. I didn't openly rebel against or resent God; instead I just felt forgotten.

Your life experiences may cause you to feel as these people did. But let me assure you that God will never be a father who comes home drunk, hides behind a newspaper, beats you, molests you, lies to you, betrays you, deserts you, or is too busy for you. He is different. He is a father who "knows the things you have need of" (Matt. 6:8) and will "give good things to those who ask Him" (Matt. 7:11). He will never leave nor forsake you, He will unfailingly have your best interest in mind, and He will always have more for you than you ever dreamed of for yourself.

Think about your relationship with the heavenly Father as you read through the statements in the box below.

A LOOK AT YOUR RELATIONSHIP WITH YOUR HEAVENLY FATHER

See if any of these statements apply to you:

- "I doubt that I am a beloved son or daughter of my heavenly Father."
- "I feel distant from Him."
- "I am afraid of Him."
- "I am angry with Him."
- "I feel abandoned by Him."
- "The thought of my heavenly Father brings tears of pain rather than feelings of joy."

If any one of the statements in this box applies to you, you definitely need a greater understanding of your heavenly Father's love for you. Ask Him to make it clear. Pray the prayer at the end of this chapter. And then determine that you will not close yourself off from the Father who loves you. Give Him a chance to prove Himself faithful and show His power in your behalf.

Read through His words to you in the box below and write your name on the blank lines.

A MESSAGE FROM YOUR HEAVENLY FATHER

Hear God speak directly to you when He says in the Bible:

"I will be a Father to you, _____, and you shall be My sons and daughters" (2 Cor. 6:18).

And when He says:

"Do not fear, _____, for it is your Father's good pleasure to give you the kingdom" (Luke 12:32).

In my new relationship with God, I was strongly aware of His love, especially His love for other people, but I didn't believe that He loved me as much as He loved them. The enormity of residual hurt and unforgiveness from the past, along with guilt, sadness, and fear, all served as a giant barrier that kept me from feeling His love. Because of these things, acknowledging God as Father took a great step of faith.

You may have a distorted image of God because of everything that has happened to you, but you will not be able to see who you really are until you are able to see God as He really is. Then, out of the context of a relationship that secures and satisfies you, you can begin to grow.

If you want to begin this process, or to renew your relationship with your Heavenly Father, say one of the following prayers:

Prayers

To Know God as Your Heavenly Father

God, I acknowledge You as my heavenly Father today. Heal any misconception I have of You. Where my earthly father has failed me and I have blamed You, forgive me and take away that hurt. I long to receive the inheritance that You have promised Your children.

To Renew Your Relationship with God as Father

If you know God as your father, but feel distant from Him at times, pray the following prayer:

Lord, I know You are my heavenly Father and You love me as no one else can. But sometimes I cannot feel Your unconditional love for me. Help me understand the truth of Your Word in my life today. And help me draw closer to You.

Chapter Five

IS THE HOLY SPIRIT REAL?

WHEN I FIRST HEARD THE NAMES HELPER AND COMFORTER in reference to the Holy Spirit, I knew immediately I wanted those attributes of God in my life. I realized that to get them, I first had to acknowledge the Holy Spirit's existence and then be open to His working in me. When I did that, I learned three important reasons to be filled with God's Holy Spirit:

- to worship God more fully
- to experience and communicate God's love more completely
- to appropriate God's power in my life more effectively

If you acknowledge Jesus as Savior and God as Father, you have to acknowledge the Holy Spirit. I've heard certain Christians speak of the Trinity as Father, Son, and H-H-L-L-S-S-P-P-S-S-H-H. They can hardly say "Holy Spirit" without choking, let alone acknowledge His working in their lives. Perhaps it's because they know too little about Him. Or maybe they were in a situation in which odd things were done in the name of the Holy Spirit. (Or perhaps they heard the term "Holy Ghost" and were afraid of ghosts!)

One day after my initial meeting with Terry and Pastor Jack, I was browsing in a Christian bookstore and came across Joanne Marxhausen's charming children's book *Three in One*. The author used the example of an apple with its three parts—the peel, the flesh, and the core—to point out that those three parts were still just one apple. Likewise, she described three aspects of God: the Father, the Son, and the Holy Spirit. Three parts, but only one God.[1] The message of this simple illustration was so clear that I realized we can never truly know God until we know Him in all those ways.

There are five ways the Holy Spirit works with us, which I have noted in the box below.

THE WORK OF THE HOLY SPIRIT

1. *He reaffirms God's love for us.* In Paul's letters to the churches, he is trying to help other Christians grow spiritually. He knows what has been essential in his relationship with the Father, and he wants others to experience that same blessing. Paul first introduces the ministry of the Holy Spirit in chapter 5 of the book of Romans. He says, "Now hope does not disappoint, because the love of God has been poured out in our hearts by the Holy Spirit who was given to us" (v.5).

2. *He gives us the power to do what is right.* Paul struggled with the same temptations that we do every day. In Romans 7:15 he confesses, "For what I will to do, that I do not practice; but what I hate, that I do." Like us, Paul cannot fully overcome the

temptation to sin. The Holy Spirit is mentioned nineteen times in Romans 8 as Paul searches for an answer to his dilemma. Then he says, "For if you live according to the flesh you will die; but if by the Spirit you put to death the deeds of the body, you will live" (Rom. 8:13).

3. *He prays for us.* God has sent the Holy Spirit to help us when we don't know what words to say. Paul says, "Likewise the Spirit also helps in our weaknesses. For we do not know what we should pray for as we ought, but the Spirit Himself makes intercession for us with groanings which cannot be uttered" (Rom. 8:26).

4. *He teaches us the words of Christ.* The disciples had many questions for Jesus as he prepared them for His coming death at the Last Supper. Knowing that He was leaving them, they tried to reconcile all they had been taught into some kind of theology. Jesus knew they would need more than that. He promised them that "the Helper, the Holy Spirit, whom the Father will send in My name, He will teach you all things" (John 14:26).

5. *He gives us insight into future events.* At the Last Supper, Jesus went on to assure the disciples that the Holy Spirit would give them insight into the future. "When He, the Spirit of truth, has come . . . He will tell you things to come" (John 16:13).

Aren't we all looking for this kind of help in our own lives?

The Holy Spirit cannot be ignored. We can't pretend He doesn't exist or say that Jesus didn't mean it when He promised He would send the Holy Spirit to us, or suggest that God was just kidding when He said He was pouring out His Spirit on all humankind. The Holy Spirit is not a vapor or a mystical cloud; He is another part of God. The Holy Spirit is God's power and the means by which God speaks to us. If we ignore or reject Him, we will cut off this power and communication from working in our lives.

If your lips can say, "Jesus is Lord," you can be sure the Spirit of God is working in your life already. Being filled with the Spirit is mentioned in many Scriptures. Since there seem to be just as many interpretations of them as there are denominations, I'm not going to confine you to mine. Simply ask the Holy Spirit what those Scriptures should mean to you, and leave it in His hands to tell you.

WHAT WOULD JESUS SAY?

Jesus described the Holy Spirit to His disciples in this way:

"If you then, being evil, know how to give good gifts to your children, how much more will your heavenly Father give the Holy Spirit to those who ask Him!" (Luke 11:13).

Jesus also spoke about the Holy Spirit right before He ascended into heaven. He told His disciples:

"And I will pray the Father, and He will give you another Helper, that He may abide with you forever—the Spirit of truth, whom the world cannot receive, because it neither sees Him nor knows Him; but you know Him, for He dwells with you and will be in you" (John 14:16–17).

These words are just as true for us today.

How about you? If you think you don't need the Holy Spirit in your life, ask yourself the questions below:

1. Would you like to feel God's love for you?
2. Do you need help living God's way and in making the right choices?

3. Would you like to always know how to pray about your life?
4. Do you need a teacher to help you understand God's Word and Christ's teachings?
5. Would you like insight into future events?

If you answered yes to the above questions, you are looking for the power of the Holy Spirit in your life.

Over the years I have discovered that the infilling of the Holy Spirit is ongoing and ever deepening. We have to be willing to open up to each new level and dimension so that He can enable us to accomplish what we could never do without this full measure of His love, power, and life.

No matter how long you have known the Lord, it's good to pray the following prayer to Him frequently:

Prayer

God, help me understand all I need to know about You and the workings of Your Spirit in my life. Fill me with Your Holy Spirit in a fresh new way this day, and work powerfully in me.

Chapter Six

HOW DO I GIVE GOD CONTROL OVER EVERY AREA OF MY LIFE?

ONCE I'D BEGUN TO KNOW GOD AS SAVIOR, AS FATHER, and as Holy Spirit, I found I needed to expose many areas of my life to His influence. This was difficult because it called for my deepening trust. Until then I'd had few positive experiences when someone other than myself was in control of my life.

In every house I lived in when I was growing up, we always had rooms that no one was allowed to see. They contained a confusing clutter of items rendered useless by their overwhelming number and lack of order. One reason my mother never wanted anyone to come to our house (aside from the fact that it was too exhausting for her to keep up a front of normalcy) was that she was afraid someone would see the secret rooms. These rooms were reflective of our family life. The secret of my mother's mental illness had to be hidden at all costs. When I grew up, it was as if those secret rooms in our home became secret places in my heart. I kept so many parts of me hidden that I lived in terror that they would be discovered and I'd be rejected.

When I first received Jesus into my heart, I showed Him into the guest room. The problem was, He wasn't content to stay there. He kept knocking on one door after another until I was opening doors to rooms I had never even known were there. He exposed every dark corner of each room to His cleansing light. I soon realized that He wanted me to acknowledge Him as Lord over every area of my life.

One such room in my heart was the issue of having children. I married my husband, Michael, about three years after I received Jesus, and because so much was happening in our lives at that time, we never really discussed children. I had a million reasons for not wanting any, not the least of which was the fear that I would perpetuate my own crippled upbringing. I couldn't bear to watch myself destroy an innocent life.

As God knocked on one door after another—finances, marriage, attitudes, appearance, friendships—I opened up to His lordship. Yet I turned a deaf ear as He tapped relentlessly at the door of motherhood, which was dead bolted by my selfishness and fear. The knocking persisted, however, challenging my daily "Jesus, be Lord over every area of my life" prayer.

One morning about a year after we were married, friends stopped us before church to show off their new son. As I held him briefly, I had a vision of holding a child of my own. Later in church I thought about that moment, and the possibility of having a baby suddenly seemed pleasant.

Okay, Lord, I thought, *if we're really supposed to have a child, let me hear something to that effect from Michael.* With that I put the matter totally out of my mind.

Later that afternoon, Michael turned to me and said, "That baby you were holding this morning before church was so cute. Maybe we should have one of our own."

"What?" I said in disbelief. "Are you serious?"

"Sure. Why not? Isn't that what people do?" he asked.

"Yes, but I've never heard you say anything like that before."

Remembering my quick prayer that morning, I prayed silently, *Lord, it's frightening how fast You can work sometimes. May Your perfect will be done in my life.*

Even though I was still fearful and apprehensive, I knew the time had come when God was going to bring life to a place in me that had died years before. I sensed that allowing Him to be Lord over this area would be a major part of the redemption of all that had been lost in my life.

GIVING HIM THE RUN OF THE HOUSE

When you invite Jesus into the home of your being (being born again), you are supposed to also give Him the run of the house (making Him Lord over your life).

WHAT WOULD JESUS SAY?

If you asked Jesus, "Do you really want me to give you the run of the house?" He would answer:

"You shall love the LORD your God with all your heart, with all your soul, and with all your mind" (Matt. 22:37).

However, many of us are slow to give the Lord complete control of our lives. Whether we admit it or not, we hesitate to believe that God can be trusted with every area.

Yet the Bible says,

> Trust in the LORD with *all* your heart,
> And lean not on your own understanding;

In all your ways acknowledge Him,
And He shall direct your paths.
(Prov. 3:5–6, emphasis added)

Notice that word *all*. It's very specific. If we want things to work out well, we have to acknowledge Him as Lord over *all* areas of our lives. I had to be willing to give God the right-of-way by frequently saying, "Jesus, be Lord over every area of my life." Then as He pointed to places where I had not opened the door to His rulership, I let Him in.

I know now that God does this with all people who invite Him to dwell in their lives. Some young people give Him total access to the home of their being right away. Others leave Him standing in the entryway indefinitely. Many teens do as I did and allow Him to gain entrance slowly. When He knocks on different doors inside you, just know that He will never bulldoze His way in and break down the walls. He will simply knock persistently and quietly and, as He's invited, gently occupy each corner of your life to clean and rebuild.

When my husband and I lived in California, we had a house that was open, with few walls on the inside. People would tell me, "When I come into your house, I can't just stay in the entryway. I have to walk into the living room, kitchen, or den." Because of the lack of barriers, the home itself invited them to move through it. I believe this reflects the way our relationship with God is supposed to be. When the barriers are down, He is not restricted from going into any area He desires. That means we are open to whatever God wants to do in us, no matter how uncomfortable it may feel at the time. The happiest people I know put all of their lives into God's hands, knowing that wherever He is enthroned, no threat of hell can succeed against them.

Acknowledging God as Lord over every area of your life is an ongoing act of will. Because of that, I recommend saying a short prayer like this every morning when you wake up:

Prayer

God, I acknowledge You as Lord over every area of my life this day. Help me walk in Your perfect will in all that I do and everything that I say.

Chapter Seven

DOES GOD CARE ABOUT MY NEEDS?

A FEW WEEKS BEFORE I HAD THAT TALK WITH TERRY about meeting her pastor, I woke in the middle of the night choking back sobs and gasping for breath. Feelings of desperate loneliness swept over me like that of being lost in the dark as a child, and I had a sense of some strange overpowering and suffocating, deathlike presence in the room with me. I jolted to a sitting position to see, much to my relief, that I was safe in my own bed.

"Thank God, it's not real," I cried into my hands as I tried to massage away memories of the all-too-familiar dream.

Part of the emotional torment of the years before I came to the Lord was recurring nightmares so genuine that when I awoke from them it took time to determine what was reality and what was not. In these frightening dreams, I was in a big, dark, empty room that grew larger and larger until I was overwhelmed and engulfed with paralyzing fear. The gripping despair I felt from these nightmares became so intense that gradually it carried over into the daytime as well.

When I shared these events with Terry, she gave me what seemed at the time to be very odd advice.

"When that happens," she instructed me, "just speak the name of Jesus over and over. It will take the fear away."

"That's it?" I replied, doubtful yet willing to do anything she said if it would help. We had not discussed the Lord much before, so this suggestion seemed very foreign.

I didn't think much about our conversation until the next time I woke out of a nightmare and immediately remembered Terry's advice.

"Jesus," I whispered as I gasped for air. "Jesus!" I called louder and held my breath for a moment. "Jesus, Jesus, Jesus," I said again and again as though clinging for life to the sound of that word. In a few minutes the fear lifted.

It's just as she predicted, I thought to myself in amazement as I rolled over and went back to sleep.

That was my first experience with the power of Jesus' name, and I have never forgotten it. If His name had that much effect over the realm of darkness for someone who was not even acquainted with Him, imagine the power of His name for those who know and love Him.

A NAME FOR ALL SEASONS

Certain guarantees and rewards are inherent in simply acknowledging the name of Jesus. For example, the Bible says, "The name of the LORD is a strong tower; the righteous run to it and are safe" (Prov. 18:10).

There is a covering of protection over anyone who turns to the name of the Lord. That's why my saying His name over and over—not in a mindless chanting but crying out to Him for help—brought the kingdom of His life to bear upon mine. It's true I had not at that point received Him as Savior, but I was being drawn to Him, as the events of several weeks later proved.

The Lord has many names in the Bible, and each one expresses an aspect of His nature or one of His attributes. When we acknowledge Him by those names, we invite Him to be those things to us. For example, He is called Healer. When we pray, "Jesus, You are my Healer," and mix it with faith, it brings this attribute to bear upon our lives.

A NAME TO ANSWER EVERY NEED

Do you need hope? He is called our Hope (Ps. 71:5). Pray, *"Jesus, You are my Hope."*

Are you weak? He is called our Strength (Isa. 12:2). Pray, *"Jesus, You are my Strength."*

Do you need advice? He is called Counselor (Ps. 16:7). Pray, *"Jesus, You are my Counselor."*

Do you feel oppressed? He is called Deliverer (Ps. 70:5). Pray, *"Jesus, You are my Deliverer."*

Are you lonely? He is called Immanuel, which means "God with us," our companion and friend (Matt. 1:23). Pray, *"Jesus I count you as my Friend."*

God is not some distant, cold being with no interest in you. He is Immanuel, the God who is with you right now to the degree you acknowledge Him in your life.

A NAME TO ANSWER EVERY NEED

Jennifer Rundle knew God's power to answer her every need. As a high-school senior, she looked forward to graduation activities at her Virginia Beach school. A popular teenager, she wanted to celebrate this milestone in her life with her friends—by joining them at prom, graduation parties, and summer days at the beach. But the sharp pain in her abdomen, which had begun five years earlier, was crippling on some days. She had been going to doctors for the problem, but the only definite diagnosis had been anemia, which had been treated.

Then Jennifer and her mom noticed a lump on her side that seemed to come and go. Her mom called her aunt, who was a doctor, and she advised them to see a gastroenterologist, who quickly ordered a new round of tests at a local hospital.

This time the diagnosis was clear: Jennifer had a malignant tumor growing in her colon—almost unheard-of in someone her age. Surgery would be scheduled immediately.

"Surgery?" Jen asked her parents and the doctor. "I won't need surgery," she said. "Jesus will heal me."

Jennifer was admitted to the hospital and prayed fervently to keep up her faith. She knew God could heal her, and she and her parents prayed daily for a healing. Her dad helped her search the Bible for God's promises about healing, and she taped them to her hospital-room wall, one above the other, so the doctors and nurses and every visitor who entered the room could not help but comment on the unusual wallpaper.

Still, the days went by, and Jennifer's condition remained unchanged. Surgery loomed ever closer. *Why,* Jen wondered, *is God taking so long with my miracle?*

Three days before her surgery, Jennifer was sitting on her hospital bed, praying with her parents.

"What's wrong with what we're praying?" Jen asked her parents. "What's wrong with our faith? Why have I not been healed?"

"I don't know," her dad admitted.

So they decided to change the focus of their prayers. Instead of asking God to heal Jennifer, they asked, "What do You want to do, Lord?"

That was a revolutionary step for Jennifer. As they prayed for God's guidance in her situation, the words from Ephesians 3:20–21, verses she had memorized in Bible study, consumed her mind: "Now to him who is able to do immeasurably more than all we ask or imagine, according to his power that is at work within us, to him be glory in the church and in Christ Jesus throughout all generations" (NIV). It was as if God was speaking to her directly.

She opened her eyes and told her parents. "I know what the Lord wants to do," she said. "The Lord just said two things. First, He wants to do more than we are asking or imagining. And second, He wants us to pray that He will be glorified."

Suddenly Jennifer became grateful for her circumstances. No longer would she put God in a box; God was about to do something important through this—even if it meant she had to have an operation.

Word of Jen's condition spread. People in the hospital began asking Jennifer and her family about their faith. Doctors, nurses, and patients all heard the gospel, and many accepted Christ. The local newspaper picked up her story and ran an article, complete with photographs of Jennifer and her patchwork wallpaper. Four follow-up pieces later, Jen found herself deluged with visitors, calls, and letters—many from people she had never met.

On May 13, 1983, four days after her eighteenth birthday, Jennifer had surgery to remove the tumor, which had grown to the size of a grapefruit and was nestled against an artery. Positioned as it was next to some lymph nodes, the cancer had had every opportunity to spread throughout her bloodstream—particularly since it had festered undetected for five years. To the doctors' amazement, though, they could find no traces of the cancer in her blood or anywhere else in her body. The nature of cancer is to grow, but as they put it, "Somehow, this tumor contained itself."[1] The doctors were able to remove all of it.

God had answered her prayers for healing; He had performed

a miracle in this battle with cancer. Her sister, Jodi Berndt, tells Jennifer's story in her book *Celebration of Miracles*, which recounts a number of miraculous stories—from a missionary surrounded by murdering bandits to a baby faced with a life-threatening tumor. And even in their diversity the miracles proclaim a common and unmistakable message: God knows our needs, and He is willing and able to meet them.

Reflecting on God's goodness, Jennifer made a startling observation: "Even with the physical pain, this has been one of the best times in my life."[2]

Another good reason to acknowledge the name of the Lord is that Jesus says if we acknowledge Him, He will acknowledge us. And there is an intimacy that grows as long as this acknowledgment is sustained.

IN ORDER TO KNOW HIM BETTER

When my mother locked me in the closet for hours at a time, I felt helpless and afraid. "They've forgotten me," I cried to myself. "No one remembers I'm here." So it wasn't surprising when I later became fearful that God would forget me too. I felt as King David did: "For there is no one who acknowledges me; refuge has failed me; no one cares for my soul" (Ps. 142:4).

Sometimes we feel that no one knows or cares who we really are. But God knows and cares. One common question from people who have been abused is, "Where was God when the abuse happened?" The answer is that God is where He is asked to be. He knew and cared that I was locked in that closet. Yet it wasn't until years later when I asked Him that He released me and healed me of its effects. It would have happened sooner if I had received Him and made Him Lord over my life.

No matter who has deserted or failed us in one way or another in the past, the Lord will always be there for us today. The Bible says, "When my father and my mother forsake me, then the LORD will take care of me" (Ps. 27:10). Those words are particularly meaningful if your mother or father has, in fact, abused, disappointed, or forsaken you. The Lord, however, will never let us down or forget us.

Jesus said when you know the truth, you will be set free. I always thought that meant knowing the truth of a situation, but actually it is knowing *God's* truth in every situation. And our eyes will never be opened to His truth until our hearts are fully opened to Him and we acknowledge Him as everything we need. For that is God's will for our lives.

Prayers

Jesus, thank You that You are Immanuel, God with us. Thank You that You are with me and You care about my needs.

Mention your needs and then refer to any of the names of God that apply. For instance, "You are my Overcomer [John 16:33] and I need You to help me overcome my loneliness." Or "You are my Patience [Rom. 15:5] and I need patience today with _____."

I thank You that You are there for me in this way. Please help me sense Your presence in a new way today.

Part Two

HOW CAN I FOLLOW
GOD EACH DAY?

Building a Solid Foundation

Chapter Eight

HOW DO I
GROW SPIRITUALLY?

"I'M STILL ON SHAKY GROUND," I SAID TO MYSELF AS I drove to church one Sunday morning nearly a year after coming to know the Lord. Even though my life was much improved, I still had this uneasy feeling that at any moment I could lose the stability I'd gained. I feared that my glimpses of hope for the future would all come to nothing.

It was obvious that I had made *some* progress since that day in October with Terry and Pastor Jack. After all, in the beginning of my relationship with the Lord, I wasn't even able to get myself to church. For months Terry and her husband woke me on Sunday mornings with a phone call and then drove out of their way to pick me up, knowing I wasn't strong enough in my mind, body, or spirit to get there on my own.

After they stopped taking me, my attendance was sporadic for a time until I resolved to get myself to church regularly without their assistance. Now as I was driving myself there for the fifth consecutive Sunday morning, I thought about what I had been learning.

I'd heard Pastor Jack preach every week about "moving on with the Lord," and it was finally starting to register. Each time he mentioned it, he waved his arm slowly across the congregation, like a shepherd trying to move his sheep in a certain direction. One morning as he waved his arm over the congregation, I realized that you don't just stay in one place after you receive the Lord. You have to start growing.

I had thought that after you received Jesus into your life, that was it. You'd made it. No more problems. But I was finding that wasn't the case. The truth is, I *had* made it into eternity by securing life after death. However, my life here on earth still needed work. I had to do certain things daily to sustain life and become spiritually and emotionally healthy. What a revelation!

Having pursued physical fitness and the concept of proper body care for many years, I quickly related to this discipline—doing something good for yourself, no matter how much you didn't *feel* like doing it, so that you would be able to enjoy good health and well-being. I began to understand that just as the physical body needs to be fed, exercised, and cleansed, so the spirit and soul need replenishing.

> When the whirlwind passes by, the wicked is no more, but the righteous has an everlasting foundation.
>
> PROVERBS 10:25

That morning in church I thought, *My foundation isn't as strong as it should be. That must be why I have times of doubt and feel like I'm on shaky ground. God, show me how to strengthen my relationship with You so that my foundation becomes solid.*

Over the next few months I learned about five key elements—spiritual building blocks—that will strengthen our relationship with God:

1. The Word of God
2. Prayer
3. Praise
4. Confession
5. Ongoing forgiveness

By neglecting even one of them, we end up with cracks in our foundation. When we have cracks in our foundation, we never end up where we are supposed to be and we can never fully know God's will.

An Excerpt from Rachel Scott's Journal

I stand back, God, and I watch those around me and ask myself, What is it that they're feeling? What is it that they're thinking? Are they seeing you? Can they hear you? If so, why can't I? What am I doing so wrong that I can't reach that level? Everyone looks at me and thinks, Wow, what a together kinda girl. She's doing good. But you know, God, that I'm not. Why won't you fix that? I don't understand. This feeling is killing me, God. Why don't you do something? I know that you have already done so much, but why stop there? I want to reach a new level with you, God. Take me there. I want that so much. I want to serve you. I want to be used by you to help others. But I feel like I can't do that until you change this feeling I have. Come to me, God, and make use of me.

Your Servant,
Rachel Joy[1]

Some people do "get by," never doing any of these key elements I mentioned, but I wasn't interested in getting by any more than Rachel Scott was. I'd been doing that for years. I wanted true spiritual well-being and a sense of purpose and direction. I wanted God's will for my life.

Prayer

Lord, help me remember the importance of Your Word, prayer, praise, confession, and ongoing forgiveness in my daily walk. Help me not neglect any one of them. Open my mind and heart to walk even deeper with You in each of these areas.

Chapter Nine

IS THE BIBLE RELEVANT
TO MY LIFE?

ONE MORNING AS PASTOR JACK ONCE AGAIN ENCOURAGED us to "move on," this time in the Word of God, I thought, *First Pastor asks us to bring our own Bibles; now he wants us to read them ourselves?* I had purchased a Bible in a translation that I could understand, just as he had requested, but I thought that he would teach us from it and we would follow along.

Years before I had given up trying to read the Bible when several unsuccessful attempts brought discouragement and frustration. I found the writing so foreign, I couldn't understand it at all. But Pastor Jack taught from the Scriptures with amazing clarity, and I hung on every word. It was like watching a movie so reflective of my own life that I became involved in the action.

Could it be, I asked myself, *that I might feel that same way when I read the Bible at home alone?*

The next morning I began reading in Psalms and Proverbs,

which had short chapters and seemed to be safe enough for me to tackle. Over the following weeks I branched out into the gospels of Matthew, Mark, Luke, and John. I was surprised at the way every word came alive with new meaning. (Could that be the power of the Holy Spirit in my life, teaching me all things as the Scripture says?) Soon I had such a desire to know the whole story that I started at the beginning of the Bible and read straight through to the end. When I finished months later, I felt as if I knew the heart of the Author and my life had been changed.

While I was reading semifaithfully each day, I noticed distinct and undeniable benefits. I discovered it was especially beneficial to read Scripture the first thing in the morning because it set my heart and mind on the right course for the day. Also reading the Bible before I went to bed at night ensured that I would sleep without nightmares, which had been a problem for as long as I could remember.

Gradually the Bible became God's voice in my ear. When I heard certain old, familiar words in my mind, such as *You're worthless. You'll never amount to anything. Why try?* I also heard the words of God saying, *You are fearfully and wonderfully made. I will lift you up from the gates of death. You will be blessed if you put your trust in Me* (Ps. 139:14; 9:13; 2:12).

The more I read, the more I saw that God's laws were good. They were there for my benefit, and I could trust them. It became clear to me that conscience wasn't an adequate indicator of right or wrong. I could see that things really can only be found right or wrong in the light of God's Word. Such guidelines, rather than restricting, were actually liberating to me.

WASHED BY THE WORD

Christian singer Rebecca St. James tells what God's Word means to her in her devotional book, *You're the Voice: 40 More Days with God:*

Ten minutes ago I was out in the garden planting some potatoes with some friends. Now I have to tell you, when you plant potatoes, you get rather messy! My hands were absolutely covered with packed-on dirt! Praise God for water and soap! This relates to an analogy I want to share with you. One day while I was reading Ephesians 5, it really struck me that if we are not in the Bible, we are not cleansed. The Bible convicts us, challenges us, and shows us where we are dirty. It shows us where we need to clean up our lives. When we don't get into the Word daily, we are continually getting filthy. What a challenge to "wash up"![1]

Even when God's Word did not specifically say, "This is right" or "This is wrong," my spirit became so aligned with His that I could sense what was correct. For example, while the Bible did say not to be drunk, I no longer felt it was even a good idea for me to drink alcohol for a "relaxed" feeling, especially in light of my history of alcohol and drug abuse. Besides, the "high" I was getting from being in the presence of the Lord was far greater than any I could derive from other sources. This was just one of many beginning signs of emotional maturity and wholeness that were being worked in my soul, the foundation of which was laid in the Word of God.

WHAT? ME, READ?

You may be thinking, *I can't afford the time it takes to read the Bible every day.* Let me challenge you to reconsider. In the box below I have listed five reasons to read the Bible daily. After you read this list, you will realize that we can't afford to let a day go by without absorbing at least a few verses of the Word into our hearts and minds.

FIVE REASONS TO READ THE BIBLE

The theme of Psalm 119, which is the longest psalm and the longest chapter in the Bible, is: God's word is true and wonderful. In this psalm the psalmist answers the question "Why should I read the Bible daily?"[2]

1. *So I can shape myself and my life correctly.* The second stanza of Psalm 119 begins with a question: "How can a young person stay pure?" And the answer is, "By obeying your word and following its rules" (v. 9 NLT). The author goes on to say, "I have hidden your word in my heart, that I might not sin against you" (v. 11).

2. *So I can have strength, comfort, and hope.* The fourth stanza of Psalm 119 describes our condition: "I lie in the dust, completely discouraged" (v. 25). The antidote? God's Word. The psalmist pleads with God, "Revive me by your word . . . I weep with grief; encourage me by your word" (v. 25, 28).

3. *So I can distinguish good from evil.* In the thirteenth stanza of Psalm 119 the writer claims to have more insight than his teachers because "I have refused to walk on any path of evil, that I may remain obedient to your word" (v. 101). The Bible can help all of us—young and old alike, Bible teacher and student, layman and clergy—to separate good from evil in our daily lives.

4. *So I can have direction and know God's will.* The fourteenth stanza of Psalm 119 begins with a familiar verse: "Your word is a lamp for my feet and a light for my path" (v. 105). Just as we need a flashlight to see at night, we need God's Word to light our way in a dark world.

5. *So I can be rid of anxiety and have peace.* The psalmist says, "Powerful people harass me without cause" (v. 161), one reason he has been deprived of peace. Only four verses later he assures us, "Those who love your law have great peace and do not stumble" (v. 165).

Reading God's Word must become a daily discipline because we need a solid grasp of the way God intends us to live if we are going to live for Him. Spiritual wholeness requires some sacrifice and discipline, just as good relationships, good health, and being good at what you do all require sacrifice and discipline. The Bible says, "Man shall not live by bread alone, but by every word that proceeds from the mouth of God" (Matt. 4:4). Regular feeding on God's Word satisfies the hunger of our souls and keeps us from emotional depletion and spiritual starvation. It also keeps us in the center of God's will.

Perhaps you wonder as I did at one point, *How can I be sure that the Bible is really God's Word?* I reply to that question by asking another: "How can you be sure it isn't?" The only way you can know about a book for certain is to read it straight through. You can't judge the Author unless you've read His book.

Don't let other people be the only way you hear or read about what God's Word says (even if they are great Bible teachers like Pastor Jack); read it for yourself, keeping in mind that it was written for you. Get up early to read the Bible in the morning, if at all possible, in order to set the tone for the day. If you can't read then, decide when you can. Lunch hour? After school? After dinner? Before bed? Make this an appointment with God and write it down on your calendar.

THE TESTIMONY OF THOSE WHO HAVE GONE BEFORE

The apostle Paul, who at one time persecuted Christians, told the Hebrew Christians about the importance of God's Word in his life. He said:

"For the word of God is living and powerful, and sharper than any two-edged sword, piercing even to the division of

soul and spirit, and of joints and marrow, and is a discerner
of the thoughts and intents of the heart" (Heb. 4:12).

And centuries before **David, the giant killer and later king of
Israel,** spoke of the ministry of God's Word in his life:

"The testimony of the LORD is sure, making wise the simple;
The statutes of the LORD are right, rejoicing the heart;
The commandment of the LORD is pure, enlightening the
eyes" (Ps. 19:7–8).

If the version of the Bible you're reading is difficult to understand, get another translation. I have used the New King James
Version, the New International Version, the New Living Translation,
and the New Century Version in this book. If you can't afford to
buy a more readable translation, ask around for one. Make a bold
request of your youth pastor. There are people all over the world
who would like nothing better than to give you a Bible if you just
let them know your needs.

WHAT IF I'M HURTING?

At times in my battle with fear and depression, I sat down to read
the Word of God feeling so depleted, numb, or preoccupied, I
could hardly even comprehend the words. I not only didn't feel
close to God, but I felt it was futile to hope He could ever change
me or my life in any lasting way. In spite of that, as I read I was
struck by a remarkable lifting of those negative emotions.
Afterward I may not have been able to pass a quiz on the passage,
but I felt renewed, strengthened, and hopeful.

When you feel fearful, depressed, or anxious, take the Bible
in hand and pray the prayer at the end of this chapter. Then

begin to read God's Word until you sense peace coming into your heart.

While the Bible was written to give you knowledge of the Lord, it takes the Holy Spirit to bring a particular Scripture alive to your heart. When that happens, take it as God speaking words of comfort, hope, and guidance directly to you. The apostle Paul said, "For whatever things were written before were written for our learning, that we through the patience and comfort of the Scriptures might have hope" (Rom. 15:4).

WHAT WOULD JESUS SAY?

If you asked Jesus, "Is it important for me to read the Bible?" He would answer:

"If you abide in Me, and My words abide in you, you will ask what you desire, and it shall be done for you" (John 15:7).

The Bible is God's love letter to you. When you receive letters from someone you love, you don't just read them once and never look at them again. You pore over them time after time, drinking in the very essence of that person, looking between the lines for any and every possible message.

These love letters to you are full of messages. They say, "This is how much I love you." They do not say, "These are the things you need to do to *get* Me to love you." The Bible is not just a collection of information; it is a book of life. It's not to be read as a ritual or out of fear that something bad will happen if you don't. It's to be read so that God can build you up in His love from the inside out and brand His nature into your heart so that nothing can keep you away from His presence or out of His will.

Prayer

Lord, I thank You for Your Word. Reveal Yourself to me as I read it and let it come alive in my heart and mind. Show me what I need to know. Let Your Word penetrate anything that would block me from receiving all You want to say to me today.

Chapter Ten

IS THERE POWER IN PRAYER?

DURING THE FIRST COUPLE OF YEARS I WALKED WITH
the Lord, my prayers went something like this:

- "God, help me get that job."
- "Jesus, please heal my throat."
- "Father, take away my fear."

It took me a while to realize that those spur-of-the-moment
prayers were not accomplishing much. I thought I should do the
best I could on my own, and then if I needed a lifeline from God,
I could grab for it. The only problem was, I needed a lifeline every
other minute.

I loved the Scripture that says, "Ask, and it will be given to you;
seek, and you will find; knock, and it will be opened to you"
(Matt. 7:7). I took God at His word and was asking, seeking, and

knocking on a pray-as-you-go basis. I also took to heart the Scripture that says, "You do not have because you do not ask" (James 4:2). *Great! I can easily remedy that*, I thought, and I proceeded to ask for everything. But I was still not happy, and I didn't see the kind of answered prayer I desired.

One day as I was again reading that same verse, my eyes were opened to the next verse: "You ask and do not receive, because you ask amiss, that you may spend it on your pleasures" (James 4:3). Could it be that the "God-give-me-this, do-that, wave-your-magic-wand-here, get-me-out-of-this-mess" kind of praying was not what God desired for my prayer life? In utter frustration I said, "Lord, teach me how I'm supposed to pray."

He did exactly that!

I came to understand that prayer is not just asking for things—although that certainly is part of it. Far more important, prayer is talking with God. It's getting close to and spending time with the One you love. It's taking the time to say, *Speak to my heart, Lord, and tell me what I need to hear.*

Still later I came across the Scripture that says, "For your Father knows the things you have need of before you ask Him" (Matt. 6:8). This puzzled me, so I questioned Pastor Jack: "If God already knows what I need, why do I even need to ask for anything?"

IF GOD ALREADY KNOWS, WHY DO I NEED TO ASK HIM?

In his usual clear manner, Pastor Jack explained, "Because God has given us a free will. He has set it up so that we always have a choice about everything we do, including whether or not we choose to communicate with Him. He will never intervene where man does not want Him."

Of course! I thought. *God wants us to desire to be with Him. There* is no love relationship if one person has to dictate how the other must think, feel, and act.

"God knows our thoughts," Pastor Jack continued, "but He *responds* to our prayers. We have to come to a place of realizing that prayer is a privilege that is always ours, but the power in prayer is always *His*. *Without God, we can't do it. Without us, God won't do it.*"

That put a whole new perspective on the subject. Things wouldn't happen in my life unless I prayed. And I was no longer just asking for things; I was partnering with God. I was aligning my spirit with His, and together we would see that His perfect will would be done.

One significant example of this was my prayer for a husband.

PRAYING FOR THE RIGHT PERSON

I had been married when I was young, before I became a believer, but after the failure of that short marriage, I seriously doubted I could ever be happily married. It was what I wanted most, but it wasn't until I started praying about it that I began to have hope.

Lord, is there someone with whom I can share my life? I prayed. *Someone I can love without being rejected? Someone who loves You and me and will be faithful to both of us?*

I had only been praying that prayer a short time when I started dating Michael Omartian, and I was desperately afraid of making another mistake. But God had taught me how to pray about such matters, so that's what I did.

"Lord, I thank you for Michael," I prayed every day, "but if he is not the husband You have for me, take him out of my life. Close the door on our relationship. I don't want to live my way any-more. I want Your will to be done in my life. I seek You first, knowing You will provide all that I need."

The more I prayed that prayer, the closer Michael and I

became, until finally we were both certain we were to be together. In all the years we've been married, neither of us has wondered if we married the wrong person, even during the toughest times. That's because our relationship was covered and committed to God in prayer from the beginning.

HOW TO PRAY EFFECTIVELY

We have to learn that we can't leave our lives to chance. We have to pray over anything that concerns us, no matter how big—"With God nothing will be impossible" (Luke 1:37)—or how small— "The very hairs of your head are all numbered" (Matt. 10:30).

If you have any doubt about the importance of prayer, or if you are still praying on an on-again/off-again basis, go through the six reasons to pray in the box below.

SIX REASONS TO PRAY

1. *To seek the face of the Lord and get to know Him better.* "When You said, 'Seek My face,' my heart said to You, 'Your face, LORD, I will seek'" (Ps. 27:8).

2. *To unburden your heart.* "I cry out to the LORD with my voice; with my voice to the LORD I make my supplication (Ps. 142:1).

3. *To make your requests known to God.* Jesus said that, "whatever things you ask in prayer, believing, you will receive" (Matt. 21:22).

4. *To hear God.* God said, "Blessed are those who keep my ways" (Prov. 8:32).

5. *To resist temptation.* Jesus told His disciples, "Watch and pray, lest you enter into temptation" (Matt. 26:41).

6. *To receive God's reward.* Jesus said, "pray to your Father who is in the secret place; and your Father who sees in secret will reward you openly" (Matt. 6:6).

Do whatever you have to do to secure a place and time to pray. When I was single and during the first few years of marriage, that was not a problem. However, after our first child was born it was much more difficult. When our second child arrived, the only way I could spend time with the Lord was to get up at 5:30 A.M. The only place I could go at that hour and not disturb anyone was a small walk-in closet off the master bath.

What a contrast to my early years of being locked in the closet for punishment! Now I went there to commune with God. This went well for a while until I was discovered. First I was visited regularly by my eighteen-month-old daughter, who learned to climb out of her crib and come looking for me. Soon her six-year-old brother followed her.

One morning, when both of them, plus my husband, two dogs, and several hamsters, ended up in the closet, I knew it was time to either get up earlier or find a new location. Sometimes we have to revise our plans, but securing a time and place to be alone with God is worth any effort.

Without reducing prayer to a formula, I found that it is good to include certain key points in each prayer time:

- Tell the Lord how much you love Him.
- Thank Him for all He has done for you.
- State how dependent you are upon Him.
- Tell Him everything that's in your heart.
- Confess anything that needs to be confessed.
- Give Him all your requests.
- Wait for Him to speak to your heart.
- Praise Him for working powerfully in your life.

Don't ever feel inhibited because you think you can't pray. If you can talk, you can pray. And don't be concerned about prayer talk, church talk, or Christianese talk. The Bible tells us the only qualifications we need: "He who comes to God must believe that He is, and that He is a rewarder of those who diligently seek Him" (Heb. 11:6). We just have to believe that He is a good God.

DOES GOD ALWAYS HEAR MY PRAYERS?

You can never be disqualified as a person of prayer, so don't be discouraged by negative voices like, *You're not good enough to come before God's throne*, or *You've failed again, so don't go crying back to God.* Lies, lies, lies! Don't listen to any of them.

Picture a Father who never works late, never ignores or rejects you, is never too busy, and is always waiting for you to come and talk with Him. And even though you have many brothers and sisters, you are never in competition with them because He has no favorites. I know that kind of love is hard to receive if you've never been loved like that as a child, but that's your heavenly Father's availability for you. As Pastor Jack Hayford so succinctly puts it, "Your heavenly Father is waiting to hear from you. Call home!"

THE TESTIMONY OF THOSE WHO HAVE GONE BEFORE

Those who knew Jesus believed there was power in prayer.

James, the half-brother of Jesus, didn't believe Christ was the Savior until after Jesus' crucifixion. Then he became one of the leaders of the early church. He told them:

"The effective, fervent prayer of a righteous man avails much" (James 5:16).

The apostle Peter also spoke about the power of prayer in his life. He said:

"For the eyes of the LORD are on the righteous, and His ears are open to their prayers (1 Peter 3:12).

Don't allow discouragement over unanswered prayer to cause you to doubt that God has heard you. If you have received Jesus and are praying in His name, then God hears you, and something is happening whether you see it manifested in your life now or not. In fact, every time you pray, you're advancing God's purposes for you. Without prayer, the full purpose God has for you can't happen.

POWER IN NUMBERS

It's important to understand that spiritual well-being depends upon two kinds of regular prayer. One is deep, intimate prayer alone—just you and God. The other is prayer together with other believers—praying for one another. The battle to confront temptation and stay in the center of God's will becomes far too difficult to fight entirely alone. We need others praying with us to give us strength, to help us think straight, to lift our vision above our circumstances.

There is power in two or more people praying together because God's presence attends it. This is one of His promises, and when He promises something, He doesn't *try* to keep His promises, as you and I do; He *keeps* them. I don't believe you can find complete spiritual well-being unless people are standing with you in prayer.

WHAT WOULD JESUS SAY?

If you asked Jesus if you should find a friend to pray with you, He would answer:

"Where two or three are gathered together in My name, I am there in the midst of them" (Matt. 18:20).

He would also say:

"And whatever things you ask in prayer, believing, you will receive" (Matt. 21:22).

My friend Diane, whom I led to the Lord, had been my best friend since high school. Because we had similar dysfunctional family situations, we understood each other's prayer needs and fell into the habit of praying regularly together over the phone several times a week. It was actually easier to pray for her than it was to pray for myself, because there was no end to the possibilities I could see for her. (I have found that you can pray only so much for yourself without getting bored or frustrated because of being too close to your own situation.) Our prayers for one another were instrumental in our spiritual growth.

Gradually my prayer partners increased from one to three, then five, and eventually seven. These groups met in my home every week for years. My husband, Michael, and I also had a number of couples meet with us to pray on a monthly basis. With that many people united in prayer for one another, someone is praying for each member all the time. I can't imagine facing life without that support.

When my family and I moved to another state, we had to start all over again because we didn't know many people. But we were blessed in that my sister, Suzy, and her family and my close friend, Roz, and her family moved to the same town at the same time. They had been part of my prayer group for years. This was not a coincidence. I believe God was in the center of their decision, just as He was in the center of ours.

Right away, Suzy, Roz, and I started our prayer group with just the three of us. At first I thought, *Lord, will our prayers be powerful enough with only three people praying? Yet I know You say that when two or three are gathered together in Your name, You will be in the midst of them. We need You desperately to be in our midst every day.*

In those early days we prayed for God to send new members to our prayer group. We prayed for our families. Our church. Our neighborhoods. Our community. If one of us was sick, the other two would be there in prayer. If one of us was weak, the other two would hold her up in prayer. We were grateful for the strength of one another's prayers, and we became more and more dependent on God for every step we took. We each agreed that we didn't know how we could survive that difficult transition without those prayers.

Everyone needs one or more persons with whom they can pray and agree every month, every week, or every day if need be. You need that too. This must go two ways, though. You must be praying for them, also. Don't be afraid, shy, or hesitant to take this crucial step. Ask God to lead you to at least one other believer, and be bold enough to ask that young person if he or she wants to pray with you regularly.

If the first person you ask can't do it or it doesn't work out, don't feel rejected or get discouraged; just keep looking for the right one. And don't hesitate to pray for someone's requests because you fear your prayers won't be answered, as I did in the beginning. *Remember, your job is to do the praying; it's God's job to answer the prayers.*

Whether you pray with others or you pray alone, it's beneficial to read the Word of God before you pray because it prepares your heart to pray according to God's will. Have a pencil and paper with you so you can write down anything the Lord speaks to your heart. Or keep a diary or journal as Rachel Scott did. If you need an ability to pray beyond your own capabilities because you are too weak, too upset, or too frightened, ask the Holy Spirit to help you.

Once you pray about something, put it in God's hands. That doesn't mean you don't pray about it again; it just means that you have laid that burden at the Lord's feet. The answer will always come, although it might not be in the way you expect or according to your timing. Most important, you have spent time in the Lord's presence, where you can hear God speak to you about His will for your life.

Prayer

Lord, I know there is power in prayer, and I have a deep desire to draw close to You in prayer. Help me rise above the distractions and busyness that rob me of those times with You. Help me make prayer a priority so that I can learn what Your will is for my life.

Chapter Eleven

WHY DO I NEED TO PRAISE GOD?

"I CAN'T DO IT!" I CRIED TO GOD IN PRAYER SHORTLY after Michael and I were married. "I can't handle the dishes. I can't handle the house. I can't handle my work. I can't handle the loneliness of being a wife of someone who works all the time. I can't deal with my own emotional ups and downs, let alone my husband's! I can't do any of it, God, not any of it!"

I wept before the Lord with a mixture of frustration and guilt over the fact that I was feeling this way about my husband, my home, and my life. God had rescued me and given me hope and a future. How could I—who knew what it was to be hungry and poor and feel that there was no love or purpose in my life—tell God I couldn't handle these answers to my own prayers?

Fortunately, the Lord did not strike me with lightning; instead He waited quietly until I was finished and then softly reminded me, *You are trying to do everything in your own strength.* As I sat there in my discouragement, I sensed the Holy Spirit speaking to my heart, saying simply, *All you have to do is worship Me in the midst of what you are facing, and I will do the rest.*

"Oh, thank You, Lord," I prayed through my tears. "I think I can at least handle doing that much."

I lifted my hands and said out loud, "Lord, I praise You in the midst of my situation. Thank You that You are all-powerful and there is nothing too hard for You. Thank You for who You are and all You have done for me. I worship You, Jesus, almighty God, Holy Father, Lord of my life.

"Lord, I give You my home, my marriage, my husband, and my work. They are Yours," I said as my shoulders relaxed, the knot in my stomach left, and I sighed with tears of relief.

The pressure was off. I felt free of the burden I had been carrying, because the burden was now His. I didn't have to try to be perfect anymore, and I didn't have to beat myself up when I wasn't all I thought I should be.

Since that time, praise has become a habitual attitude of my heart that says, "No matter what is going on in and around me, *God is in charge!* I trust Him to bring good out of this situation and work things out for my highest blessing."

Praise is not always my first reaction to things, however, so I often have to remind myself of Pastor Jack Hayford's teaching on praise. He said, "It's not your saying, 'I'll give it everything I've got and the Lord will bless it,' but rather it's the Lord saying to you, 'You just bless my name and *I'll* give it everything *I* have.'" That's power in praise!

Now, when I come to the place where my flesh can't go any further, I stop where I am and worship God. This key has unlocked even the heaviest of closet doors and illuminated the darkest of nights. It frees you to get your mind off yourself and onto the Lord.

A KEY TO TRANSFORMATION

Worship is powerful because God's presence comes to dwell in our midst when we praise Him, and in His presence we find healing, transformation, and direction for our lives. In fact, the more time we spend praising the Lord, the more we will see ourselves and our circumstances grow in wholeness and completeness. That's because praise softens our hearts and makes them pliable. It also covers us protectively.

Please read the preceding paragraph again. Underline it, circle it, draw arrows pointing to it, commit it to memory, write it on your hand, or do whatever you have to do to remember it. This important truth is the first thing we forget and the last thing we remember because our flesh doesn't naturally want to do it.

WHAT WOULD JESUS SAY?

If you asked Jesus, "Is it really all that important for me to praise you?" He would answer:

"But the hour is coming, and now is, when the true worshipers will worship the Father in spirit and truth; for the Father is seeking such to worship Him" (John 4:23).

Praise and worship of God are always acts of will. Sometimes our problems or the burdens we carry choke out our good intentions, so we have to make the effort to establish praise as a way of life. Yet it only becomes a way of life when we make it our first reaction to what we face and not a last resort. That's when we find true freedom in the Lord.

Now is the time to start being thankful to God for everything in your life. Thank Him for His Word, His faithfulness, His love, His grace, His healing. Thank Him for what He has done for you personally. Thank Him for the friends He has brought into your life and for helping you to get along with others. If you have trouble thinking of something, then thank Him that you're still breathing and that you can read. Keep in mind that whatever you thank the Lord for—close friends who stand beside you or parents who love you or better grades—will start the process of that blessing being released to you.

In the Old Testament, the people who carried the ark of the covenant stopped every six steps to worship. We, too, need to remind ourselves not to go very far without stopping to worship. For our spiritual well-being, we have to be six-step persons who continually invite the presence of the Lord to rule in our situations. We have to be free to praise Him no matter what our circumstances.

A WEAPON AGAINST FUTILITY

Without praise we experience an eroding that leads to bondage and death. The Bible says, "Although they knew God, they did not glorify Him as God, nor were thankful, but became *futile* in their *thoughts,* and their foolish *hearts* were *darkened*" (Rom. 1:21, emphasis added). With praise you and your circumstances can be changed, because it gives God entrance into every area of your life and allows Him to be enthroned there.

So anytime you struggle with negative emotions, such as anger, unforgiveness, fear, hurt, depression, or worthlessness, thank God that He is bigger than all that. For instance, if you are angry with a friend, you might pray, "Lord, I don't seem to be able to get over my anger at this person, but You are all-powerful and can make it happen. I thank You and praise You for Your power in my life." Doing this is your greatest weapon against the feelings of anger or inadequacy that undermine all God has made you to be.

WORSHIP, GOD'S WAY

There are several ways to praise God that don't always come easily but are crucial to spiritual health.

1. *Praise is meant to be sung.* King David says in Psalm 147:1, "It is good to sing praises to our God; for it is pleasant, and praise is beautiful." This is often hard for us because at times singing is the last thing we feel like doing, or we're so self-conscious about our voices that we don't open our mouths, even when we're alone. Yet in the Bible the singers went before the troops into battle because their singing praise to God confused the enemy. It works exactly the same way for us today.

Many times in the early days of my walk with God, my soul was tormented with such depression in the middle of the night that I would get up, shut myself in my prayer closet so I wouldn't wake anyone, and sing softly to the Lord. I'd sing a hymn, or a chorus, or make up a song. Sometimes all I could sing was "Thank You, Jesus. Praise You, Lord," over and over until I felt the oppression leave and strength come into my soul.

You may be so depressed or hurting that you feel you can't even unclench your jaw. When that happens say, "God, give me a song in my heart that I can sing to You," and begin to hum to the Lord any melody that comes to mind. Then put words to this melody. Don't worry about the pitch, the rhythm, the melody, or the sound of your voice. Sing it all on one note if you want.

Remember, the true singer is the one who has God's song in his heart. The Lord thinks your voice is beautiful. He designed it for the purpose of praising Him. Continue to sing over your situation because, as you do, something is happening in the spirit realm and you will feel the heaviness lift.

2. *Praise is meant to be expressed with the lifting of your hands:* "Lift up your hands in the sanctuary, and bless the LORD" (Ps. 134:2). Lifting our hands to the Lord as we praise God is also an act of the

will that is not second nature to us. It is really not the strength of our arms that lifts our hands, but rather the love in our hearts.

The most important reason for you to do this is to let go of everything you're holding on to and surrender to God: "I give up, Lord." You can also think of it as taking your life in your hands and offering it up to Him: "I give You everything of myself, Lord."

An Excerpt from Rachel Scott's Journal

Rachel Scott knew how to let go of the problems she was holding on to by thanking God and praising Him. On March 2, 1998, she wrote:

Dear God,

I know that at first I was really jealous of _____. She's sweet, pretty, popular, & she got the major part of the drama. But now I only admire those qualities. You have blessed her with gifts & talents and I can only be happy for her. Thank you for giving her the lead role in the drama. It has taught me that I won't always be in the spotlight. I am thankful to have a chance to be in the drama at all. Tomorrow I have an audition. I am not expecting to get a part. If I don't, I promise not to criticize or become jealous of those who make it. If I get a part, I promise not to let it go to my head, and I will remember to thank thee, for the ability, strength, courage, & talent you blessed me with. I don't want to be successful without you, God. I can't be successful without you.

Love Always,
Rachel Joy[1]

3. *Praise is meant to be done together with others as well as alone.* "In the midst of the assembly I will sing praise to You" (Heb.

2:12). I used to hurry into the church thirty minutes late on Sunday mornings. By the time I found a seat and settled into it, the worship time was over and the pastor was preaching. I wasn't concerned about this because I was there for the teaching. Yet my mind wandered everywhere and didn't settle into the message until the sermon was half over.

On the days I arrived in plenty of time to get a seat *before* the service started and was a full participant through the entire worship time, I found I was open to receive the message as if God was speaking directly to me. My heart was made soft and receptive to what the Holy Spirit wanted to teach me because of the thirty to forty minutes I had spent worshiping God in unity with other believers. Negative attitudes I had come in with were melted away and replaced with ones more in alignment with what God desired.

Don't miss times of worship with other believers. Many negative emotions will be released from your heart in group worship, and this will protect you from all that steals your peace.

Prayer

Lord, I thank You that You are my strength. Thank You that no matter what I face at this moment, You are greater. I am grateful that You give me the knowledge and strength I need to get where I need to go. I praise You this day for who You are and for Your goodness to me.

Chapter Twelve

CAN MY SINS BE FORGIVEN?

AFTER I CAME TO KNOW THE LORD AND EXPERIENCED that warm, close, rich feeling of walking with God, I still fell back into some old, familiar bad habits. I had only known the Lord for a few months before I went out on tour with a music group. None of them were believers, and so it was easy to be drawn back into their drinking and partying lifestyle.

When I came home after a month of that decadent life, I went back to church but I didn't feel the intimacy with God that I had been experiencing before I left. I recognized that it was probably because God was not pleased with the way I had been living the past four weeks. I began to feel guilty, depressed, and hopeless about my life again.

The following Sunday, Pastor Jack talked about the damage unconfessed sin can do to your soul. I knew that God was talking to me. Right there in church I quietly confessed to the Lord my sinful actions of the past month. The moment I did, I felt that wonderful sense of God's love again, and I couldn't stop the tears from flowing.

Here I had been thinking that God had turned His back on me, but the truth was that my actions had separated me from Him. I hated that feeling of being distant from God, and I vowed to never let unconfessed sin come between me and the Lord again. I would try my best to live His way, but if I failed, I would confess it immediately so I could receive His forgiveness and not lose the close fellowship with Him that I had come to treasure so dearly. I knew my sins would be forgiven.

THE WEIGHT OF UNCONFESSED SIN

When sin is left unconfessed, a wall goes up between you and God. The agony of unconfessed sin is accurately described in the Bible by King David:

> When I refused to confess my sin,
>> I was weak and miserable,
>> and I groaned all day long.
> Day and night your hand of discipline was heavy on me;
>> My strength evaporated like water in the summer heat.
>> (Ps. 32:3–4 NLT)

Even though the sin may have stopped, if it hasn't been confessed to the Lord, it will still weigh you down, dragging you back toward the past you are trying to leave behind and keeping you from moving into the future God has for you. I know because I used to carry around a bag of failures on my back that was so heavy I could barely move. When I confessed my sins, I actually felt the weight being lifted.

Often we fail to see ourselves as responsible for certain actions.

For example, while it's not your fault that someone hurt you, your reaction to it is your responsibility. You may feel justified in your anger or bitterness, but you still must confess it because it misses the mark of what God has for you. If you don't, its weight will eventually crush you.

For confession to work, repentance must go along with it.

THE KEY IS REPENTANCE

Repentance literally means to turn your back, walk away, and decide not to do it again. It's possible to confess without ever really conceding any fault at all. In fact, we can become simply good apologists with no intent of being any other way. Confession and repentance mean saying, "This is my fault. I'm sorry about it, and I'm not going to do it anymore."

THE TESTIMONY OF THOSE WHO HAVE GONE BEFORE

Solomon, the last king of Israel, who was known for his wisdom, said this about confession:

"He who covers his sins will not prosper, but whoever confesses and forsakes them will have mercy" (Prov. 28:13).

And Paul, that renegade who once persecuted Christians, said:

"There is no creature hidden from His sight, but all things are naked and open to the eyes of Him to whom we must give account" (Heb. 4:13).

All sin has to be confessed and repented of for you to be free of bondage, whether you feel bad about it or not and whether you recognize it as sin or not. The Bible says, "My conscience is clear, but that does not make me innocent" (1 Cor. 4:4 NIV).

Every time you confess something, check to see if you honestly and truly do not want to do that anymore. And remember, God "knows the secrets of the heart" (Ps. 44:21). Being repentant doesn't necessarily mean you will never do it again, but it does mean you don't intend to do it.

If you have committed a sin that you just confessed the day before, don't let that come between you and God. Confess it again. As long as you are truly repentant each time, you will be forgiven and eventually you will be completely set free. The Bible says, "Repent therefore and be converted, that your sins may be blotted out, so that times of refreshing may come from the presence of the Lord" (Acts 3:19).

Because we are not perfect, confession and repentance are ongoing. There are always new levels of Jesus' life that need to be worked in us. Therefore we need to also confess our hidden faults.

CONFESSING HIDDEN FAULTS

When you are building a foundation, you have to dig out the dirt. The trouble is, most of us don't go deep enough. While you can't see all your errors all the time, you can have a heart that is willing to be taught by the Lord. Ask God to bring to light sins you are not aware of so that they can be confessed, repented of, and forgiven. Recognize that there is something to confess every day and pray frequently as King David did:

> And see if there is any wicked way in me,
> And lead me in the way everlasting. (Ps. 139:24)

Create in me a clean heart, O God,
And renew a steadfast spirit within me. (Ps. 51:10)

Cleanse me from secret faults. (Ps. 19:12)

Sometimes when we don't think we have anything to confess, praying for God's revelation will reveal an unrepentant attitude, such as criticism or unforgiveness, that has taken root in our hearts. Confessing it keeps us from having to pay the emotional, spiritual, and physical price for it. It will also benefit our social lives since the imperfections in our personalities, which we can't see, are often obvious to others.

After King David confessed his sins in Psalm 32, he felt this relief:

I said to myself, "I will confess my rebellion to the LORD."
    And you forgave me! All my guilt is gone. . . .
Many sorrows come to the wicked,
    but unfailing love surrounds those who trust the LORD.
So rejoice in the LORD and be glad, all you who obey him!
    Shout for joy, all you whose hearts are pure! (Ps. 32:5, 10–11 NLT)

An Excerpt from Rachel Scott's Journal

October 15, 1998

Jesus, break these strongholds
Tear down the strings of sins
Release me from my pride
Rescue me from these games
Restore me from the hurt
Renew my heart again.[1]

There is also much healing when we confess our faults to another person for the purpose of prayer. The Bible says, "Confess your trespasses to one another, and pray for one another, that you may be healed" (James 5:16). Ask the Lord to show you when it is right to do that. But choose a person who is trustworthy and won't use the information against you.

Always keep in mind that God's ways are for your benefit. Confession is not for Him to find out something; He already knows. Confession is for you to be made whole.

Prayer

Dear Lord, I know that I have sinned in this way: _____.
Forgive me for my error. It grieves me to stumble like this, and I vow to turn my back on this sin. I'm not only sorry; I am truly repentant. Help me overcome any tendency toward this in my life.

I also ask You to cleanse me from secret faults. Show me where I don't live Your way and help me correct these errors.

Lord, I don't want to miss all You have for me. I don't want to cover my sins and not prosper. I want to forsake them and live in your mercy.

Chapter Thirteen

DO I HAVE TO FORGIVE MYSELF, GOD, AND OTHERS?

I STRUGGLED WITH FORGIVING MY MOTHER FOR YEARS. Even after I became an adult she continued to be abusive, and I had to forgive her on a daily basis. Sometimes I stayed away from her and just let my dad deal with her by himself. Unfortunately she turned her anger toward him. When he became ill with a lung infection, instead of trying to help him, she would prepare her own meals and eat them in front of him without offering him anything. She said if he was hungry he could get up and get his own food.

When I found out all of this, I was very upset with her. What a turn of events! I had spent all those years trying to forgive her for being cruel to me, and now I had to forgive her for the way she treated my dad. There certainly didn't seem to be any way to change the situation. We'd tried to get my father to hospitalize my mother, but when he came to sign the papers, he couldn't do it. He still hoped that someday she would return to being the person he thought he had married.

Lord, I prayed, *I know my mother is mentally ill and doesn't really know what she is doing. But there is still something in me that thinks she does and that makes me mad. I again ask you to give me a forgiving heart toward her.*

The Lord answered that prayer time and again as each new offense brought more reasons to forgive. I know that I never could have heard God's leading for my life if my heart and mind had been clouded with unforgiveness.

STAIRWAY TO WHOLENESS

Forgiveness leads to life. Unforgiveness is a slow death. Not forgiving someone doesn't jeopardize your salvation and keep you out of heaven, but it does mean you won't enjoy all that God has for you. And you may find yourself wandering around outside the center of God's will.

The first step to forgiving is to receive God's forgiveness and let its reality penetrate the deepest part of your being. Being forgiven and released from everything we've ever done wrong is such a miraculous gift, how could we refuse to obey God when He asks us to forgive others as He has forgiven us? Easy! We focus our thoughts on the person who has wronged us, rather than on the God who makes all things right.

Forgiveness is a two-way street: God forgives you, and you forgive others. God forgives you quickly and completely upon your confession of wrongdoing. You are to forgive others quickly and completely, whether they admit failure or not. Most of the time people don't feel they've done anything wrong anyway, and if they do, they certainly don't want to admit it to you.

WHAT WOULD JESUS SAY?

If you asked Jesus, "Is it important for me to forgive _____?" He would answer:

"And whenever you stand praying, if you have anything against anyone, forgive him, that your Father in heaven may also forgive you your trespasses" (Mark 11:25).

Forgiveness is a choice that we make. We base our decision not on what we feel like doing but on what we know is right. I did not feel like forgiving my mother. Instead I chose to forgive her because God's Word says, "Forgive, and you will be forgiven" (Luke 6:37). That verse also says that we shouldn't judge if we don't want to be judged ourselves.

I had to understand that God loves my mother as much as He loves me. He loves all people as much as He loves me. He loves the murderer, the rapist, the prostitute, and the thief. And He hates all of their sins as much as He hates ours. He hates murdering, raping, whoring, and stealing as much as He hates pride, gossiping, and unforgiveness.

I also had to forgive my dad. Since he wasn't the abuser, I didn't even realize I was angry toward him. But when I asked God to reveal any hidden unforgiveness, rage surfaced in me over the fact that he had never once let me out of the closet, and he had not protected me from my mother's insanity. I had always felt he was never there for me. I cried longer and harder over that than I had ever cried before, and afterward I felt a giant weight had been lifted from my shoulders. I had always loved my dad, but that day set me free to love him more. We see a person quite differently once we've forgiven him or her.

THE TESTIMONY OF THOSE
WHO HAVE GONE BEFORE

The apostle Peter knew about forgiveness. He watched as the Romans killed his friends for following Christ. Yet he was able to say:

> "Let all bitterness, wrath, anger, clamor, and evil speaking be put away from you, with all malice. And be kind to one another, tenderhearted, forgiving one another, even as God in Christ forgave you" (Eph. 4:31–32).

Before my dad died, he spent six years living with our family and was a great blessing to all of us. Not only was he an avid encourager of my children and an enthusiastic sports companion for my husband, but he was *always* there for me in a way that has been remarkably healing. He loved to cook and cooked wonderful meals for us when I was too busy to do it. He kept an eye on the children if I had to leave. He took care of many household chores that I hated—especially cleaning out the fireplace and taking out the trash. I don't believe this living arrangement would have worked so successfully if I hadn't been willing to forgive.

Forgiving your parents is one of the most important things you can do. One of the Ten Commandments, which are not ten suggestions but ten commandments, says, "Honor your father and your mother, that your days may be long upon the land which the LORD your God is giving you" (Ex. 20:12). Forgiving them is part of that honoring and will affect the length and quality of your life.

Pastor Jack Hayford said something that affected me profoundly with regard to forgiving my own mother. He said, "You grow up to hate yourself when you hate your parents because what you see of them in yourself you will despise." When you despise something in yourself, check to see if it's because it reminds you of one of your parents. If so, there may be an area of unforgiveness there.

We may sit and compare our sins to other people's and say, "Mine aren't so bad," but God says they all stink, so we shouldn't worry about whose smell the worst. The most important thing to remember when it comes to forgiving is that *forgiveness doesn't make the other person right; it makes you free.*

When I say the word *forgiveness*, what is your response? Read the statements in the box below and see if they reflect the way you have felt or feel today.

FORGIVENESS IS A CHOICE

Read through the statements below and mentally check those people you might need to forgive.

I can't forgive my mom or dad. They always put me down.

I can't forgive my friend who hurt me by telling lies about me behind my back.

I can't forgive my sister (or brother). She (he) has always been my parents' favorite.

I can't forgive the family member who abused me.

I can't forgive _____, who revealed something I told this person in confidence.

I can't forgive _____ because _____.

As bad as what that person did to you, can you choose to forgive him or her? Remember, forgiving this person does not necessarily make him or her right; it makes you free.

And don't be surprised if it takes time to accomplish this

forgiveness. Beth Nimmo, Rachel Scott's mother, said, "In the year since Rachel's death, I have found it difficult to follow Christ's command to forgive the killers. Forgiveness has been a daily battle for me. Sometimes it has even been a moment-by-moment struggle. From the beginning I have asked the Lord to give me real forgiveness for Eric and Dylan, but that desire is repeatedly tested. . . .

One year after Rachel's death, forgiveness for me is not a one-time act of my will, but it's a choice I make on an ongoing basis. I choose constantly to forgive, even when I don't want to. I choose constantly to lay down my pain because I trust that God is going to do something incredibly beautiful through all this.[1]

Forgiveness is ongoing because once you've dealt with the past, constant infractions occur in the present. None of us get by without having our pride wounded or being manipulated, offended, or hurt by someone. Each time that happens it leaves a scar on the soul if not confessed and dealt with before the Lord. Besides that, unforgiveness also separates you from people you love. They sense a spirit of unforgiveness, even if they can't identify it, and it makes them uncomfortable and distant.

You may be thinking, *I don't have to worry about this because I have no unforgiveness toward anyone.* But forgiveness also has to do with not being critical of others. It has to do with keeping in mind that people are often the way they are because of how life has shaped them. I began to truly forgive my mother when I realized how difficult her childhood had been and what problems she had faced as she grew to adulthood.

One day as I was again asking God to give me a forgiving heart toward my mother, I felt led to pray, "Lord, help me to have a heart like *Yours* for my mother."

Almost immediately I had a vision of her I had never seen before. She was beautiful, fun loving, gifted, a woman who bore no resemblance to the person I knew. My understanding told me I was seeing her the way God had made her to be and not the way she had become. What an amazing revelation! I couldn't have conjured it up myself. Nothing surpassed my hatred for my mother, except perhaps the depth of my own emptiness. Yet now I felt compassion and sympathy for her.

In an instant I put together the pieces of her past—the tragic and sudden death of her mother when she was eleven, the suicide of her beloved uncle and foster father a few years later, her feelings of abandonment, guilt, bitterness, and unforgiveness, which contributed to her emotional and mental illness. I could see how her life, like mine, had been twisted and deformed by circumstances beyond her control. Suddenly I no longer hated her for it. I felt sorry for her instead.

Being in touch with the heart of God for my mother brought such forgiveness in me that when she died, I had absolutely no bad feelings toward her. Although her mental illness and irrational behavior had continued to worsen, which kept us from any kind of reconciled relationship, I harbored no bitterness, and I have none to this day. In fact, the more I forgave her, the more the Lord brought to mind good memories. I was amazed that there were any at all.

We all need to remember that God is the only one who knows the whole story, and therefore we never have the right to judge.

FORGIVING YOURSELF AND GOD

While forgiving others is crucial, forgiveness is also needed in two other areas. *One area is forgiving yourself.* So many of us think, *I should be achieving this; I should be this kind of person; I should have done more than I have by this time in my life.* I certainly was burdened by these kinds of thoughts.

Yet God is the only one who is perfect. We have to be able to say, "Self, I forgive you for not being perfect, and I thank You, God, that You are right now making me into all that You created me to be."

Some of us have to forgive ourselves for the mistakes we have made. Before I came to know the Lord, I wasted my life doing drugs, dabbling in the occult, and getting involved in unhealthy relationships. When I was finally able to forgive myself, I realized that God could use even those experiences for His glory. I am now able to speak into the lives of adults and young people who have committed these same errors. They see that what God has helped me to overcome is possible for them too.

Besides forgiving others and yourself, you must also check to see if you need to forgive God. If you've been mad at Him, say so. "God, I've been mad at You ever since my brother was killed in that accident." Or "God, I've been mad at You ever since my parents divorced." Or "God, I've been mad at You ever since I didn't make the team." Be honest. You won't crush God's ego. Release the hurt and let yourself cry. Tears are freeing and healing. Say, "Lord, I confess my hurt and my anger, and my hardness of heart toward You. I no longer hold that against You."

Now settle the score—with others, with yourself, and with God. Slam the book shut on these memories and look forward to better relationships, greater peace with yourself, and intimacy with God.

Prayers

To Forgive Yourself

Lord, I know that You have forgiven me for my sins of _____. I thank You for Your unconditional love and grace. I am truly repentant and wish to overcome these tendencies. Now, Father, help me forgive myself. Erase my guilt and create a new heart within me.

To Forgive God

Lord, I admit that I am upset with You because of _____. Help me see things from Your perspective. I know You are a good God and have my best interests in mind at all times. Forgive me for holding this against You. Heal me of my disappointment.

To Forgive Others

Lord, _____ has hurt me in this way: _____. I do not understand why this has happened, but I know that You want me to forgive (him/her). Help me walk in (his/her) shoes and understand what would make (him/her) do or say this. Help me be completely released from all unforgiveness.

Part Three

HOW CAN I OBEY GOD?

Learning to Walk in His Ways

Chapter Fourteen

IS THERE A LINK BETWEEN GOD'S BLESSING AND MY OBEDIENCE?

I DIDN'T WANT TO MOVE FROM CALIFORNIA TO NASHVILLE. I had a great church, great friends, and a great home. But Michael felt differently. He had been commuting to Nashville a couple of times a month to work, and he had fallen in love with the city.

But I hadn't been to Nashville in twenty years, and I hadn't fallen in love with the town, so I was resistant. "If God is telling you to move to Nashville," I said to Michael, "why can't He tell me too?"

I was praying every week in my prayer group for God to show me His will, but I had not received an answer.

Two months later, I accompanied Michael on a business trip to Nashville. When I went to our room to rest before dinner, I couldn't sleep. I sensed the Lord saying, *You are supposed to be here.*

Is this really You, Lord? I prayed.

The more I lay there, the more I was sure the Lord was saying it was His will for us to make this move.

A couple of months later, we did make the move, and we were glad we did because our house in California was destroyed by the Northridge earthquake. We were grateful that we had listened to God and obeyed Him when He gave us direction for our lives. It has been our greatest reminder that obedience and blessing go hand in hand.

BENEFITS OF OBEDIENCE

How many times do we ask God to give us what we want, but we don't want to give God what *He* wants? We lack what we desire most—wholeness, fulfillment, and joy—because we are not obedient to God.

Often we are not obedient because we don't understand that God has set up certain rules to protect us and work for our benefit. The Ten Commandments were not given to instill guilt, but as an umbrella of blessing and protection from the rain of evil. We need God's laws because we don't know how to make life work without them. The more I've searched the Scriptures, the more I've found that the Bible is full of promises for those who obey God.

GOD'S PROMISES OF BLESSING

Look at God's promises of blessing to you.

- The promise of healing: "Make straight paths for your feet, _____, so that what is lame may not be dislocated, but rather be healed" (modified version of Heb. 12:13).
- The promise that God will fight our battles for us: "Oh, that _____ would listen to Me, that _____ would walk in My ways! I would soon subdue their enemies, and turn My hand against their adversaries" (modified version of Ps. 81:13–14).

- The promise of living a long life in peace: "Let your heart keep my commands, _____; for length of days and long life and peace they will add to you" (modified version of Prov. 3:1–2).
- The promise of answered prayer: "If I had cherished sin in my heart, the Lord would not have listened" (Ps. 66:18 NIV).

Note that all of these promises have a qualifier: obedience.

There are many more promises like these, and just as many warnings of what will not happen in our lives if we don't obey. After reading them, I felt inspired to ask God to show me exactly what I needed to be doing. He was quick to answer that prayer. *Check your heart,* He said. *Are you really willing to obey? If so, those promises are there for you—and all My children.*

THE CHOICE IS OURS—THE POWER IS HIS

I've learned that God doesn't enforce obedience. We often wish He would because it would be easier, but He gives us the choice. I had to ask Him to teach me to be obedient out of love for Him and desire to serve the One who has done so much for me. If you want the same benefits, you'll have to do the same thing.

The Bible says that Noah was given new life because he did all that God asked him to do (Gen. 6:22). The word *all* seems frightening when it comes to obedience because we know ourselves well enough to doubt we can do it all. And the truth is we can't. But we *can* ask God to enable us to take steps of obedience.

For anyone who has been emotionally wounded in any way, a certain amount of healing will happen in your life just by being obedient to God. The Bible says, "He who obeys instructions guards his life" (Prov. 19:16 NIV). The more obedient you are, the more bondage will be stripped away from your life. There is also a certain healthy confidence that comes from knowing you've obeyed God. This confidence builds self-worth and nourishes a broken personality.

There are many different areas of obedience, but I have included just eight basic steps that will get you headed in the right direction:

1. Saying yes to God each day of our lives
2. Remaining separate from the world
3. Being baptized
4. Having fellowship with other believers
5. Knowing how to give ourselves away
6. Remembering Jesus' sacrifice
7. Walking in faith
8. Finding comfort in the center of God's will

These eight steps are a guideline, not a threat. Just take one step at a time, remembering that the power of the Holy Spirit in us enables us to obey God.

Prayer

God, I don't want to be a person who collapses every time something shakes me. I don't want anything to separate me from Your presence and Your love. And I really do have a heart that wants to obey. Please show me where I am not living in obedience to You, and help me do what I need to do. I don't ever want to miss Your perfect will for my life because I have foolishly not obeyed You.

Chapter Fifteen

DO I HAVE TO SAY YES TO GOD EACH DAY?

WHEN YOU WANT TO BUY A NEW CAR, AND YOU DON'T have all the money at that time, the car dealer will let you make a down payment and then make smaller payments every month until you have the car paid off. However, you can't change your mind and say, "I don't feel like making payments anymore," without losing both your down payment and the car.

The same is true of your relationship with God. To make Him your permanent dwelling place, your initial down payment consists of making Him Lord over your life. After that, ongoing payments must be made, which means saying yes whenever God directs you to do something. They are all a part of the purchase, but one happens initially and the other is ongoing (just like other payments!). The difference is that the Lord will take only as much payment from me as I am willing to give Him. And I can possess only as much of what He has for me as I am willing to secure with my obedience.

Taking the initial step of making Him Lord over our lives is the same for everyone. Saying yes to God every day is an individual matter. Theologians call this *sanctification*.

The word *sanctify* (*hagizao* in the Greek) is used twenty-eight times in the Bible. Sanctify is defined as "to make holy, purify." The process of sanctification fulfills God's goal for our lives: to make us like His Son, Jesus Christ.

RELEASING YOUR DREAMS

I always wanted to be a successful entertainer. It sounds embarrassingly shallow even to mention it now, but it was a desperate drive when I was younger. I desired to be famous and respected, never mind the fact that I possibly didn't have what it might take to attain either goal.

After I received the Lord and had been married just a few months, God clearly impressed upon my heart that I wasn't to do television or commercials anymore. I wasn't sure why, but I knew it wasn't right for me. Whenever my agent presented me with an interview I would have previously died for, the thought of it gave me a hollow, uneasy, deathlike feeling. Because the peace of God did not accompany the prospect of doing it, I turned down every job that was offered.

Yes, God, I won't do that commercial. Yes, God, I won't accept another television show. Yes, God, I won't sing in clubs anymore. Yes, God, I'll leave the agency.

WHAT WOULD JESUS SAY?

If you asked Jesus, "How important is it that I say yes to you every day of my life?" He would answer:

"If anyone desires to come after Me, let him deny himself, and take up his cross daily, and follow Me. For whoever desires to save his life will lose it, but whoever loses his life for My sake will save it" (Luke 9:23–24).

Gradually, all my work was gone. God had closed the doors and asked me to stop knocking on the ones that were not in His plan for me. The experience was scary, but looking back now I clearly see the reasons for it. Acting was an idol for me. I did it entirely for the attention and acceptance it would bring me, not because I loved the work. My identity was totally wrapped up in what I did.

For God to change that, He had to take away my means of defining who I thought I was and help me establish my identity in Jesus. He knew I couldn't be healed of my deep inferiority feelings if I was daily putting myself in a position of being judged by superficial standards.

The part we don't want to hear is that a time comes when each of us must place our desires and dreams in the hands of God so that He might free us from those that are not His will. If you've always had a certain picture of what you think you should do, you have to be willing to let the picture be destroyed. If it really is what God has for you, He will raise you up to do that and more. If it isn't, you will be frustrated as long as you cling to it.

Often the desires of *your* heart *are* the desires of *His* heart, but they still must be achieved *His* way, not yours, and you must know that it is He who is accomplishing them in you, not you achieving them yourself. *God wants us to stop holding on to our dreams and start holding on to Him so that He can enable us to soar above ourselves and our own limitations.* Whenever we let go of what we long for, God will bring it back to us in another dimension.

THE ART OF THE QUICK RESPONSE

Again, this is done a step at a time. If you can't trust God enough yet to say, "Anything You ask of me, I'll do," then keep working at it. I must admit that saying yes to God was difficult for me until I read God's words in the Scripture: "When I called, they did not listen; so when they called, I would not listen" (Zech. 7:13 NIV, emphasis added). That puts it all in perspective, doesn't it? If we want God to hear our prayers, we need to listen and respond to His voice.

> Delight yourself also in the LORD, and He shall give you the desires of your heart.
>
> PSALM 37:4

Being willing to say yes to God made me a candidate for much healing and blessing. Of course, I don't always hear Him and I don't always say yes immediately, but my desire is to do that. Saying yes to God without reservation is the first step of obedience that begins to build a successful and fulfilling life on the foundation you have laid down in the Word: prayer, confession, praise, and ongoing forgiveness.

Sanctification is a lifelong process that will not be completed until we are with Christ. Paul told the Philippians, "And I am sure that God, who began the good work within you, will continue his work until it is finally finished on that day when Christ Jesus comes back again" (Phil. 1:6 NLT).

This promise is for all of us.

Prayer

Dear Lord, help me to continually say yes to You. Help me not be afraid to trust You and Your will for my life. I want to experience everything You have for me.

Chapter Sixteen

WHAT ARE THE WORLDLY TRAPS I NEED TO AVOID?

THE FIRST TIME I HEARD DOLORES HAYFORD SPEAK, I knew Pastor Jack had inherited his gift of teaching from his mother. In a clear, gentle voice she told a story of her youngest son, Jim.

One day young Jim realized that some people have blessing upon blessing while others don't. He asked his mother, "Why do some people get all the breaks with God?"

After giving it some thought Mrs. Hayford said, "Son, those who get the breaks with God are the ones who first break from the world."

That piece of motherly advice stuck in my mind so strongly I pondered it for weeks afterward. *What exactly is the world?* I prayed to the Lord. *And how do I break away from it?*

Over the next few months of Bible study I came to see that the world is anything that sets itself against God and His ways. The

Bible says, "Whoever therefore wants to be a friend of the world makes himself an enemy of God" (James 4:4).

I knew I definitely didn't want to be God's enemy!

I also read, "Be sober, be vigilant; because your adversary the devil walks about like a roaring lion, seeking whom he may devour" (1 Peter 5:8). The Bible describes Satan as our "enemy," the "ruler of this world," and by aligning with the world's systems and ways of doing things, we are aligning with him.

In the past, I had rejected the idea of a personal devil as basically naive. Only the most foolish and ignorant people could support such nonsense. Besides, my occult practices had convinced me that evil existed only in people's minds. But the more I studied God's Word and saw its accuracy, the more I faced the reality of a dark and evil force controlling the lives of people who allow it.

How could I deny that it existed when I could see it manifested in every form of evil in the world around me? Now I realize that the foolish and ignorant people are those who deny the satanic realm. *Breaking from the world means recognizing our enemy and refusing to be aligned with him in any way.*

THE RULES OF THIS WORLD

Time and time again in the Old Testament, a king who served the Lord in all other things would not destroy the high places where pagan gods were worshiped. As a result, he and his people did not enjoy all the blessing, protection, healing, and answered prayer that God had for them. They, like us, did not clearly identify their enemy and break completely from the world.

Our enemy is Satan, the ruler of this world, who was originally created beautiful, wise, and without sin. He had access to the throne of God, but fell from this high position when he chose to exert his will over God's. No one tempted him; he decided to rebel on his own. When his rebellion led to his expulsion from God's kingdom, he set himself to oppose all that God is and does.

But Satan is limited. He cannot be everywhere, he is not able to do everything, he is not all-powerful, and he is not all-knowing. God, on the other hand, is all of those things.

What Satan and God *do* have in common is that they both have a plan for our lives, which can only be made operative if we submit to it. We don't have to fear Satan because the Bible says that "He who is in you is greater than he who is in the world" (1 John 4:4). Jesus' death on the cross has broken Satan's power, so we don't have to be intimidated by him.

There is no indication in the Bible that Satan can possibly win over God; God's power far surpasses his. The only success Satan can have comes through deception—getting us to believe he doesn't exist or that he is not our enemy, or instilling in us lies about ourselves, our situations, others, him, or God. Once we believe his lies, he controls our lives.

My friend Diane, who had been into occult practices with me, didn't want to get rid of her occult books or stop her occult practices when she accepted Jesus as her Savior. She thought she could mix a little bit of the occult with Christianity and have the best of both worlds. But the more she resisted giving up those practices, the more miserable and depressed she became. Nothing in her life seemed to be going right. She desperately wanted to have a child but couldn't get pregnant. She had difficulties in her marriage that caused her grief. She always felt that her prayers were not being answered.

I kept encouraging her to read the Bible for herself and attend church regularly. As she did, she began to see that she couldn't belong to both worlds—the devil's and God's. She had to choose one or the other. Finally she made the decision to throw away the books and separate herself from all occult associations and practices.

In the next few months after she made that decision, she and her husband began going to a Christian marriage counselor. Their relationship improved, and within a year she gave birth to her son, John. I don't think that was all a coincidence. Those two things alone were miracles in her life and she recognized them as such. Yet miracles don't happen when we have one foot inside the enemy's camp.

> Do not love the world or the things in the world. If anyone loves the world, the love of the Father is not in him. For all that is in the world—the lust of the flesh, the lust of the eyes, and the pride of life—is not of the Father but is of the world. And the world is passing away, and the lust of it; but he who does the will of God abides forever.
>
> 1 JOHN 2:15–17

Accepting the world's standards for our lives separates us from what God has called us to be. We reserve a place in our hearts to be the exception. We think, *I'm above the Lord's ways. I don't need to obey.* But that is what Satan said before he fell from heaven.

The way we combat this deception is simple. The Bible says, "Submit to God. Resist the devil and he will flee from you" (James 4:7). We need to separate ourselves from the world's habits and ways of thinking. We must tell Satan we refuse to believe his lies or do things his way. When we refuse Satan, the promise is, "The LORD will go before you, and the God of Israel will be your rear guard" (Isa. 52:12). The Lord will protect us from anything we may face ahead, and He will guard us against any dangers sneaking up from behind.

RUN A CHECK FOR HIGH PLACES

Breaking from the world doesn't require you to live like a hermit for the rest of your life. But you do have to run a frequent check on your heart to make sure that you are not too attached to the world.

A CHECK

Take a moment to think about your life, asking yourself the following questions:

- Do I judge myself by my peers' standard for beauty, acceptability, and success?
- Am I willing to ignore certain convictions I have in order to be part of the popular crowd?
- Do I let teen magazines or movies or soaps on television influence how I live?
- Am I drawn toward emulating the lifestyles of athletes and movie stars?
- Am I willing to compromise what I know of God's ways in order to gain something I want?

If you said yes to any of those questions, you are cutting off the possibilities God has for your life. God asks you, "Since you, _____, died with Christ to the basic principles of this world, why, as though you still belonged to it, do you submit to its rules?" (modified version of Col. 2:20 NIV).

God clearly instructs us, "Do not be conformed to this world, but be transformed by the renewing of your mind, that you may prove what is that good and acceptable and perfect will of God" (Rom. 12:2).

Two areas are particularly tempting for teens: drinking and sex. Let me share the views of a couple of young people with you, then you make your own decision in these areas.

DRINKING AND DRUGS

Kevin Max, one of the singers of the group d.c. Talk, admits to making mistakes in college. Eventually he got caught drinking at a party and was threatened with expulsion from Liberty University, the Christian college he was attending.

Kevin wanted to finish his education, and he wanted to make his parents proud by doing so. And he said he'd had his fill of carousing. Thankfully, the dean of men at the college believed in second chances.

"I actually put myself on a path to meet people who would help me reach my goals and keep me out of trouble," Kevin says in his book *Unfinished Work*.

> At first it wasn't easy because those fringe people that I'd been hanging out with were interesting and fun. I can remember being wasted and laughing at some dumb joke while we were cruising down the highway in somebody's junky car. The problem was, that highway didn't lead any-where. I always had an empty feeling at the end of the night, a feeling of wanting more than aimless fun. Because of my Christian upbringing, I knew that there was more to life, and I was determined to achieve the potential God had for me.[1]

And God rewarded Kevin's commitment. Not long after he returned to school, he met Toby McKeehan and Michael Tait, the other two members of the group. Together they did a demo of their music, a mix of rap and rock. Toby kept sending out that demo to Christian record companies and before long they had a record contract. In the years since, d.c. Talk has minis-tered to millions of teens in this country and sold millions of records.

Kevin turned his back on his desire to drink and do drugs. Other Christian teens, like Rachel Scott, have stayed away from this temptation entirely.

An Excerpt from Rachel Scott's Journal

April 15, 1998

Dear God,

I promise that I will not drink this Friday when I go out with _____. This is so tempting. I want to go so bad. Well, I thought about it (as you know) and I thought that since you would forgive me anyways I may as well do it. Then I realized that you will always, always forgive, but you may not let it go unpunished. Then I decided not to do it strictly out of fear. Then I thought about it more, and thought that if I did it out of fear it would not be done because I loved you, I obeyed you, and I followed you. That is my reason for not going now. I know that I will always be faced with temptation, but because I love you, I obey you, and I follow you, I will not fall into the core of it. Thank you, Father.

Always Your Child,

Rachel Joy[2]

SEX

When Christian singer Rebecca St. James was sixteen years old, she heard about the "True Love Waits" movement at a rally in Peoria, Illinois. At that time she felt a passionate tug on her heart to be sexually abstinent until her wedding day. Since then she has talked about virginity and encouraged other young people to stand with her and wait.

She even wrote a song, "Wait for Me," to express this concept.

A LETTER TO REBECCA ST. JAMES

Rebecca received many e-mails and letters from young people as she expressed her views about sex and sang the song "Wait for Me." Here is one letter:

My parents had always told me to wait until I was married. Although I had kept this desire alive in my heart, I somehow got lost along the way. When I was seventeen years old, I started dating a non-Christian, and I thought I had really found true love. After some time, though, I guess he was bored with me, so he decided to break up with me. I was so afraid of losing him that I told him I was ready to give myself to him. He was shocked, and tried to talk me out of it (he had known how important waiting was for me), but I just told him I didn't care anymore. I told him I really loved him and that I was sorry he hadn't felt satisfied with me.

So in my bedroom I had sex with him. I just kept telling myself over and over again that I wasn't really doing what I was about to do. My entire body went numb—*I didn't feel a thing!* I closed my eyes tightly and waited for what seemed like hours. I tried to act normal and happy, and tried to pretend that I had enjoyed the experience as well. I felt sick, and I just wanted him to go away. After he left, I just stayed under the covers and thought that I could never pray to God again because I had just turned my back on Him. The next day I called up my boyfriend and told him I didn't want to see him again. . . .

The girl went on to say that it had taken her a long time to forgive herself and accept God's forgiveness; then she closed by saying, "Making love is something so worthwhile to wait for, and I know it can only be beautiful inside of marriage."[3]

If you have already had sexual relations, like this girl, it's not too late to make a change. Teens who have had sex are deciding to make a new commitment to wait until marriage. They are choosing second virginity.

In her book *Wait for Me* Rebecca cautions teens from believing that "everybody's doing it." She gives some interesting statistics.

EVERYBODY'S DOING IT?

If you believe "everybody's doing it," consider these facts:

- Over half of all high-school students have never had sex (51.6 percent).
- Seventy-eight of all fifteen-year-olds (73 percent of boys alone) have never had sex.
- If you add to the 78 percent those whose only sexual experience was involuntary, then about 84 percent of fifteen-year-olds have never had voluntary sex.
- *The Washington Times* reported that the trend toward abstinence is increasing, as evidenced by the number of "True Love Waits" commitments made each Valentine's Day.[4]

I never thought I opposed God, but I have learned that nearly everything I did before I received Jesus opposed His ways. We can make ourselves sick by being dissatisfied with what God gives us or by running after things that are not from Him. God wants to take all cravings for the world out of our hearts and replace them with a hunger for more of Jesus.

The Bible says, "Come out from among them and be separate" (2 Cor. 6:17). You can't go forward if you cling to things that separate you from God. It's a step of obedience that happens in the heart and paves the way for true spiritual well-being in the center of God's will.

Prayer

Lord, if there are things in my life that are not of You, I don't want them. Please take them away and release me from longing for them. Help me draw on You for all my needs. Teach me to recognize my enemy and give me strength to resist him. Help me turn my heart away from the world and look only to You as my source and my guide.

Chapter Seventeen

WHAT ABOUT MY FRIENDS?

ONE EVENING, YEARS AFTER WE WERE MARRIED, MICHAEL and I had a heated argument as we were getting ready to go to a friend's house for dinner. We had misinterpreted each other's intentions and said words that were hurtful and pain provoking. I was reduced to tears and he to silence.

Great! I thought. *The last thing I want to do feeling like this is be with other people.* I silently ran through a list of reasons we could possibly cancel, but they sounded too feeble so I resigned myself to the evening.

During the entire drive to our host's home we sat in silence, except for Michael's asking, "Are you not going to speak to me all night?" To which I cleverly replied, "Are you not going to speak to *me* all night?"

I started thinking about the couple we were going to visit. Bob and Sally Anderson were one of the first Christian couples Michael and I had befriended after we were married. We had a lot in common, including our children. Their daughter, Kristen, and our son, Christopher, were born about the same time and had become good friends. We loved being with them because they were solid in their relationship as well as their faith, and we knew there weren't going to be any weird surprises in store for us.

From the moment we arrived at their home I felt the tension between Michael and me dissipate. Throughout the evening our hearts softened, and by the time we went home we were laughing. It was as if the goodness of the Lord in the Anderson family had rubbed off on us and we were strengthened by it.

This kind of thing happened so many times that when Pastor Jack exhorted us to "be in fellowship with other believers" and waved his hand across the congregation as if to get his sheep moving, I understood the need for it.

MORE THAN JUST FRIENDSHIP

The word *fellowship* sounded strange and "churchy" when I first heard it. It reminded me of tea and cookies after a missionary meeting or a potluck dinner in the church basement. I've since discovered it's much more than just coffee hour. The dictionary definition is "companionship, a friendly association, mutual sharing, a group of people with the same interests." In the biblical sense, it's even more than that.

"Fellowship has to do with a mutuality in all parts of your life," Pastor Jack taught us. "You bear one another's burdens and fulfill the law of Christ. You pray for one another, you love one another, you help one another when there is material need, you weep with those who weep and rejoice with those who rejoice. It's growing in an association with people who are moving in the same pathway you are and sharing with each other in your times of victory or need or your times of trial or triumph. It's growing in relationship."

Fellowship is instrumental in shaping us. The Bible says that we become like those we spend time with, and good friends sharpen one another just as iron sharpens iron (Prov. 27:17). This is reason enough to spend time with other believers, but there is even more to it.

AT CHURCH

First and most basic of all, it is very important that you find a church home and spend time with that body of believers in church. I certainly understand if you have been hurt or burned out by a church, but please hear me out. No two churches are alike. Each has its own personality. Some are great, some good, and some not quite what you hoped they'd be. Somewhere there is a church that is right for you, and you need to ask God to help you find it.

Contrary to what some people think, the church doesn't have to have a fancy building. You can find a good church wherever a group of believers meet with a pastor who is *also* submitted to *other* pastors and godly leaders. They must believe the Bible is the Word of God and offer good, solid teaching from it. Obviously the church you attend should have a good youth group that meets regularly and has opportunities for Bible study and prayer.

> Let us think about each other and help each other to show love and do good deeds. You should not stay away from the church meetings, as some are doing, but you should meet together and encourage each other.
>
> HEBREWS 10:24–25 NCV

You might ask yourself a few other questions. Is there an opportunity for an occasional youth retreat? Do the kids who attend there act as Jesus would want them to? A few years ago some young people and adults wore bracelets with the initials

WWJD on them. These initials stood for What Would Jesus Do. Are the teens in this church acting as if they are asking this question every day at home and at school?

The next important indication of a good church is that you sense the love of God there and you receive it in abundance from the people. Some churches make an outgoing display of love, yet others who are more reserved may be just as genuine. If you pick up feelings of pride, competition, selfishness, self-righteousness, or coldness, determine whether that is the overall atmosphere or an isolated case. Remember that in any church you could find someone to exemplify these traits.

Ask yourself if you *generally* feel love and acceptance there. You also need to be aware that you can't go into a church and *demand* that people love and care for you. You can communicate your needs, but you can't dictate how others should relate to you.

If you attend a youth group or go to a church that doesn't believe in being born again or being baptized, you need to find a church that does. If the pastor can't bring himself to talk about the Holy Spirit working in power in your life and the members of the congregation don't praise and worship the Lord, you haven't found the right place yet. God can't work as powerfully in a church that limits Him and doesn't practice certain basic steps of obedience. Continue to look until you've found a solid church you can call home.

If you are in a church where you're miserable, get out. It's hard to receive God's love and life from a church you detest. This is not license to stop going to church or "church hop" whenever the pressure to grow is on, but don't fall for the "Now we gotcha!" trap either. Leave any church that tries to control your every breath.

Ask God to lead you to the right place. When you find it, make a commitment to stay and watch yourself grow. Go as often as you can. If youth group and Sunday service once a week feel like a major commitment, start there. If this is easy, then go to midweek services also.

When you make friends with people who follow the Lord, there is a strong bond of love that makes other relationships seem shallow. Such friendships are the most fulfilling and healing.

FRIENDS ARE FRIENDS FOREVER

Many schools use Michael W. Smith's song "Friends Are Friends Forever" during graduation activities. I wonder how many notice that this song adds a qualifier to the statement that friends are friends forever. The qualifier: "if the Lord's the lord of them." That's because this song was written for a member of the Smith's Bible study and worship group. Bill Jackson was moving to another city, and the Smiths wrote the song to express the group's sadness that this man was leaving—and their joy that they would always be friends, despite the distance that would separate them. The lyrics also make it clear that the Smiths could say good-bye to this man because they knew he was going to be in God's hands. Debbie and Michael Smith's love for this fellow Christian was so strong that this beloved song was written in less than an hour.

That's the kind of friendship that can be found when Christians get together.

Sometimes friendships can be also frustrating because we expect *Christians* to be perfect when in reality only *Christ* is perfect.

It's helpful to think of all fellowship with Christian teens as beneficial: the pleasant encounters are *healing* and the unpleasant ones are *stretching*. Some teens tend to be sarcastic. When you run across kids who stretch you more than you feel you can handle, don't turn away from God. Remember, He is still perfect and good even if some of His children aren't. God always loves and respects

you, even if a few of His offspring don't. A certain person may
always leave you feeling depressed, angry, insecure, frightened, or
hurt. When that happens, it is best to let the friendship go and
give it to God to restore or remove as He sees fit.

I know that nothing hurts worse than a wound inflicted by a
brother or sister in the Lord. Having been wounded many times
like that myself, I am forced to remember that we will be imperfect
until we go to be with Jesus. So we need to be merciful to those
who "stretch" us and forgive quickly. Besides, we are probably
stretching others ourselves.

FRIENDSHIPS OUTSIDE CHURCH

Many communities around the country have Young Life groups
that have weekly club meetings for Christian fellowship. These
meetings combine songs, humor, and group interaction to create
an hour of energetic fun where kids can express that teenage tendency to push the limits—but within the controlled context of a
safe environment. The clubs for high-school students are called
Young Life clubs; the clubs for middle-school and junior-high students are called Wyldlife.

Young Life also runs camps across the United States. There you
might ride horses, go rock climbing and rappelling, take a dip in
a hot springs pool, learn to water ski or parasail, or challenge
yourself on a ropes course or a thrilling zip line. To find out about
either a local club or a camp, you can go to their Web site at
www.younglife.org.

FRIENDSHIPS WITH TEENS WHO
ARE NOT CHRISTIANS

The Bible says we should "not be unequally yoked together with
unbelievers" (2 Cor. 6:14), but this doesn't mean you have to

avoid them. It just means that your closest relationships, the ones that deeply touch and change your life, need to be teens who believe as you do. Ask yourself, *Am I a godly influence in the lives of my unbelieving friends?* If so, then consider the relationship good. However, if they influence you away from God and His ways, then cut off the relationships immediately. Remember how Cassie Bernall's friend Mona influenced her.

REBECCA TALKS

In her devotional for teens, *You're the Voice: 40 More Days with God,* Christian singer Rebecca St. James told this story:

I remember, a few years back in youth group, playing (or watching) a particular game. One person would stand on a chair, while another stood on the floor at the feet of the first person. The person on the chair would try to pull the person on the floor up onto the chair. Unless the "floor person" was extremely helpful, making it easy for him to be pulled up, then it was pretty much impossible. (Unless, I s'pose, the person on the chair was the muscle man of the youth group!) Then, the "floor person" would try to pull the "chair person" off the chair and usually succeeded within 10 seconds.

Our youth pastor would then use that physical illustration to show that often it's easier to be pulled down by the people we hang out with than to be pulled up or encouraged by them.

When you think about it, in a way, we are yoked to our friends. When bulls are yoked (bonded together by wood), if one decided to pull another way from the rest of the team, it just doesn't work. The same goes for us. If we are "bound" to friends that are going the wrong way, as much as we don't want to go, we're still going to be driven down the wrong path. We need to be so careful concerning whom we spend the bulk of our time with because, whether we like to admit it or not, our friends majorly affect how we live our lives. As my dad says, "We are who we hang with." [1]

Start somewhere. Make a phone call to a member of your youth group and ask for prayer. Or call your pastor or the local Young Life office. Meet someone for lunch in the cafeteria and talk about what the Lord has done in your life. Open up and extend yourself in some way. For instance, you might begin by watching for new students at your school as Rachel Scott did and sitting with them at lunch.

Fellowship is a step of obedience that expands our hearts, bridges gaps, and breaks down walls. It encourages, fulfills, and balances our lives. All of this is necessary for spiritual well-being and a fruitful life in the will of God.

Prayer

Lord, I acknowledge my need for friends. I ask You to lead me to relationships whereby I might grow in You and Your will might be fulfilled in me. Show me what steps to take to see that come about.

Chapter Eighteen

HOW CAN I GIVE TO GOD AND OTHERS?

WHEN I WAS TEN YEARS OLD, I LAY AWAKE IN THE MIDDLE of a cold, pitch-black night because I was too hungry to sleep. The pangs in my stomach were magnified by the knowledge that there was no food in the house and no money to buy any. My mother was asleep in the only other bedroom, on the opposite side of the house beyond the porch, and I felt isolated, alone, and afraid.

"There's nothing to eat," I had said to her earlier that evening after I searched the tiny kitchen. All I saw in the refrigerator were half-empty bottles of ketchup and mayonnaise. She had thrown remnants of old leftovers on the table for dinner—none of which went together in any appealing way—and made no apology for the fact that it wasn't enough to sustain either one of us.

"Stop your complaining. We don't have money for food," she snapped and went back to talking to herself the way she often did for hours at a time. She hated it when I intruded on her imaginary world.

Now, as I lay in bed, my mind reeled with fear about the future. I feared I could starve to death and no one would care.

Going hungry was terribly frightening. Having to be totally dependent for life and sustenance upon someone I couldn't depend on at all bred deep insecurity. I'm sure now that my mother knew Dad would bring money when he came home, but she told me there was nothing at all to eat and no way to buy it, and that was that.

We had no friends, and Mother always made it seem as if we had no family either, since she considered them all to be her enemies. I had nowhere to turn and no one to help me. We had nothing to sell, and as far as I could see we had no prospects for making any money. I became desperately afraid for my future.

Once I was out of school and self-supporting, I handled money very carefully. I felt the weight of being entirely responsible for my life, and the horror of someday starving to death always bubbled just below the surface of my mind. After I came to know the Lord and started going to church, I put money in the collection plate according to what I had with me—a couple of dollars at first, then a five, a ten, and later a twenty. It was more like I was donating to a good cause or tipping the piano player than having any thought of actually giving to God. But when I heard Pastor Jack teach on what the Bible says about giving, I knew I had far more to learn about the subject than I ever dreamed.

> But this I say: He who sows sparingly will also reap sparingly, and he who sows bountifully will also reap bountifully. So let each one give as he purposes in his heart, not grudgingly or of necessity; for God loves a cheerful giver.
>
> 2 CORINTHIANS 9:6–7

I learned first of all that giving was actually giving back to God from out of what He had given me, and by doing so I would never lose anything. In fact, I would be enriched. I also learned that the Bible teaches we are to give a tithe (10 percent) of our income to the Lord. When I started doing that, I found that my financial blessings were greater and the drains on my finances were fewer. I found, too, that the more I gave, the less fear I had about not having enough. Because I experienced such a flow of God's blessing in my life, the thought of not giving became more frightening than giving.

Two types of giving are important: giving *to the Lord* and giving *as unto the Lord*.

GIVING TO THE LORD

We often feel we will lose something if we give. We think, *If I didn't have to give this, I would have more for myself.* But actually that attitude will cause us to lose. The Bible says that if we give to the Lord, we will have everything we need in our lives. If we don't, we won't.

When Michael and I decided to move to Tennessee, we were advised to delay our relocation until we sold our California home. But we felt absolutely certain we were to go immediately, and so we moved and bought a house in Tennessee. Soon we had double mortgages, double taxes, double heating and cooling bills. We thought we were going to be buried under the financial strain.

During those months we prayed that God would send the right buyer to us. We couldn't understand why the California house didn't sell until after the earthquake happened; then we realized that God had spared not only our lives, but He had spared the lives of anyone who would have been living in the house at that time.

Although we had earthquake insurance, it didn't cover everything and so we still lost a lot of money. But we didn't count the loss. We rejoiced that no one was injured or killed in that house. Through that whole time we continued to tithe and give as God directed us. And God took care of us over the following years and eventually restored all that we had lost.

GIVING AS UNTO THE LORD

Besides giving *to* the Lord, we need to get into the habit of giving to others *as unto* the Lord. This means we are to bless others because it blesses God—without expecting something in return. What-will-I-get-back thinking sets us up for disappointment and unhappiness, but when we give and expect nothing in return, the Lord rewards us.

> You shall surely give to him, and your heart should not be grieved when you give to him, because for this thing the LORD your God will bless you in all your works and in all to which you put your hand.
>
> DEUTERONOMY 15:10

Giving is a principle of release: "Give, and it will be given to you: good measure, pressed down, shaken together, and running over will be put into your bosom. For with the same measure that you use, it will be measured back to you" (Luke 6:38). If you need release in any area, give something away of yourself, your possessions, or your life, and you will see things begin to open up to you.

There is much to give besides money or store-bought gifts. We can give food, clothing, services, time, prayer, assistance, a ride in our car, or any possession or ability that could help someone else.

It's important, however, to ask God for wisdom and direction about giving. Once my husband and I gave money to a person in need and, instead of feeding his family and paying his rent, he spent it on drugs. We've learned to use careful discernment and seek God's guidance in giving to serve His purposes.

My mother never gave anything away, and I believe that was part of her mental and emotional illness. She hoarded everything out of fear that she would someday need it. Her closets, sheds, rooms, and garages were full of "stuff." The Bible says, "He who gathered much had nothing left over, and he who gathered little had no lack" (2 Cor. 8:15). The sheer volume of my mother's stuff rendered it unusable.

Whenever my life seems to be stalled, deliberately giving of myself always brings breakthrough. It's not that you can't receive any of God's blessings unless you give but that you can't receive all of them, so life becomes more of a struggle. Remember, it's not a matter of giving to get but of taking this step of obedience to release the flow of all God has for you. Giving releases blessings into your life that may seem entirely unrelated.

Prayers

For Giving to God

Lord, help me give the way You want me to, because I want to be obedient in this area of my life. Help me always tithe so that I am never robbing You of what is Yours. I want to live in the center of Your will so I can receive all You have for me and become all You made me to be.

For Giving to Others

Dear Lord, show me any area of need where I could give something of myself or what I have. Show me what I might release of my life into the life of another person, and help me do it.

Chapter Nineteen

WHAT DO I DO WHEN
I HAVE DOUBTS?

WHAT IF THIS JESUS THING IS ALL A HOAX? I THOUGHT to myself in horror one day nearly two years after I accepted Christ as Savior. *What if none of it's true? What if the pastor suddenly says, "This is all a joke, and you fell for it! Jesus isn't real and you're not really saved!"*

That day a wall of doubt settled around me like steel bars separating me from my future. The possibility of a life of nothingness became a temporary reality, and I panicked. *What brought this on all of a sudden?* I wondered. I struggled with that flash of doubt for days, and the more I thought about it, the more unhappy I became. I knew I had to reevaluate everything.

The conversation in my head between my faithful self and my doubting self went something like this:

What was your life like before you met Jesus? I asked myself.

I was dying inside, the doubting voice had to admit.

How did you feel? I questioned further.

Full of pain, hopelessness, and fear, I answered.

Are things better now?

Much.

What's different? my faithful self asked.

I don't feel depressed, fearful, or hopeless, I answered.

When did that change?

When I received Jesus, I started to feel better.

Your experience with the Lord was real? I asked.

Well, yes, I think so.

Then what's your problem? I asked.

The problem is I can't prove that Jesus is real.

Can you prove that He isn't?

No, the doubting voice admitted.

Well, then it looks like the choice is up to you, doesn't it? To believe or not to believe. It's your decision.

Okay, then. Weighing the quality of my life before I met Jesus against the quality of my life since then, I choose to believe Him.

Are you sure? I asked.

Yes. I have decided to follow Jesus. No turning back. No turning back.

This little scenario happened five or six times in the first ten years of my walk with the Lord. In retrospect, I believe it occurred in busy and stressful times when I had not spent enough time in the Word of God or had neglected being alone with the Lord in prayer and praise. Eventually I realized that sending a doubting spirit to torment us is one of the devil's favorite tactics.

WITHOUT A DOUBT

Our first step of faith is taken when we decide we will receive Jesus. After that, every time we decide to trust the Lord for anything, we build that faith. And whenever we decide not to trust Him, we tear it down. Faith is our daily decision to trust God.

The Bible says, "Whatever is not from faith is sin" (Rom. 14:23). How much clearer can it be? Faith is obedience. Doubt is disobedience. Faith is a gift from God because He enables us to believe, but we have to obey by building on that faith.

Scripture also says that a person who doubts is unstable in every way and cannot please God. If that's true, spiritual well-being is not possible without faith.

BUILT ON THE WORD

How do we start building faith? Once we have a little, how do we get more? The first step is to be totally open and honest about any doubt in God's ability or His faithfulness to provide for our every need. Doubt emanates from a lie of the enemy, which says God is not all-powerful. If you've listened to this lie, confess it as sin.

> Without faith it is impossible to please Him, for he who comes to God must believe that He is, and that He is a rewarder of those who diligently seek Him.
>
> HEBREWS 11:6

The next step is to fill your mind with the Word. The apostle Paul said, "Faith comes from hearing the message, and the message is heard through the word of Christ" (Rom. 10:17 NIV). Reading the Word daily, regularly submitting to Bible teaching, and speaking the Word aloud will build faith. Your heart and mouth have to be united in this. Your heart can't be saying, "God can," while your mouth says, "God can't." I believe that your mind will convince your heart as you read God's Word.

Whenever I'm afraid or doubt that my life is secure, I read the Bible until I sense God's peace in me. The more I read, the more hope I have. Then, when I pray, I'm confident that God will answer my prayers.

Even if you are not given to fear and doubt, you can be attacked by a spirit of doubt, as I was. When that happens, don't carry it by yourself. Take it to the Lord immediately. Or ask a friend who knows the Lord, or your youth pastor to pray with you if you need to.

The Bible says of the people who could not go into the promised land, "They could not enter in because of unbelief" (Heb. 3:19). Don't let that happen to you. Choose to enter in to all that God has for you by taking this important step of obedience.

> Let him ask in faith, with no doubting, for he who doubts is like a wave of the sea driven and tossed by the wind. For let not that man suppose that he will receive anything from the Lord; he is a double-minded man, unstable in all his ways.
>
> JAMES 1:6–8

Prayer

Lord, I have made a decision to follow You. I know You hear my prayers even if I don't see the answers right away. No matter what happens, I am certain that I am not without hope. I have faith, but, Lord, strengthen my faith where it is weak.

Chapter Twenty

IS IT EVER GOD'S WILL
FOR ME TO SUFFER?

AS I HAVE MADE THIS PRAYERFUL WALK TO SPIRITUAL well-being throughout the years, I have received many blessings from the Lord. One special blessing was my friendship with Diane, my friend whom I led to the Lord as we talked on the phone.

Diane and I had met in drama class in high school and immediately became good friends. We found we shared similar experiences with our mothers. As a result, we each grew up with deep fears, insecurities, feelings of being abandoned, and a severe lack of maternal nurturing. Neither of us ever brought friends home from school because we never knew what condition we would find our mothers in once we got there.

We went on to attend different colleges, but afterward we shared an apartment in Hollywood where we both pursued acting careers. We also shared the same spiritual walk. When one of us was into some occult practice or Eastern religion, the other got into it with the same enthusiasm.

After we both had received the Lord, we spent even more time together. We shared ups and downs through our marriages and the births of our children. My two children were four years apart and her son, John, was right in between them in age. So they were a happy little trio whenever they were together. In fact, our families spent every holiday together.

When John was six, Diane was diagnosed with breast cancer. Our two families were devastated. She went through one miserable operation and treatment after another, and all the while we continued to pray for her healing. But then one terrible day, our worst fears were confirmed. The cancer had spread to her glands, stomach, bones, and brain.

"I just wanted to see John grow up," Diane sobbed to me when she called to report the doctor's diagnosis.

That summer, as Diane's illness progressed, I took care of John so Diane's husband could take care of her and still fulfill his business obligations. Also, Diane was suffering terribly and she didn't want John to remember her as she was in those last days. I kept praying for God's will to be done in Diane's life. We all wanted her healed. But we couldn't stand to see the agony she had to endure hour by hour every day.

A FINAL VISIT

A few days before Diane died I went to see her in the hospital. She could hardly talk because she was extremely nauseated and in a great deal of pain. Her beautiful eyes were almost expressionless. I put a cool cloth on her forehead, gave her some pieces of ice for the dryness in her throat, and applied a lip balm to her parched lips.

Then I asked her if she had written a letter to John. We had talked about this in the last few months, but Diane had been hesitant to do it. I knew why. The letter was so final. It meant that she knew she was dying, and she wanted to do everything she could to avoid facing that possibility. But this time she nodded that she had indeed written the letter and she told me where to find it.

> Blessed be the God and Father of our Lord Jesus Christ, the Father of mercies and God of all comfort, who comforts us in all our tribulation, that we may be able to comfort those who are in any trouble, with the comfort with which we ourselves are comforted by God.
>
> 2 CORINTHIANS 1:3–4

Years ago when John was born, Diane and her husband had asked me if I would agree to take care of him if anything ever happened to them. I, of course, said yes, and John was left to us in their will. That day in the hospital she asked me again. I assured her I would always take care of him.

John was eight when Diane died. For months after her death I kept him with us during the week. Early Monday morning his dad would bring John to us and then return for him on Friday night. I always hated to see him go.

The following year, John and his dad moved to Oregon where his dad could work out of his home and be with John full-time. We missed them, but we were still able to see them every holiday and summer vacation for the next few years.

ANOTHER TRAGEDY

Then one afternoon, I received a phone call from the Oregon police. John's dad had been killed in an automobile accident, and at the age of sixteen John was an orphan. How our hearts broke for him again.

That fall John became our spiritually adopted son, and I became his legal guardian. He had always been like a brother to my children and he had been like my own son. Now the relationship was official.

How blessed we were to have him as part of our family. God knew we needed someone to complete our family. We all loved him, but I especially cherished him because he reminded me so much of his mom. He had her intelligence and wit, as well as some of her mannerisms and expressions.

Through all of this, I have learned that having painful and difficult things happen to you doesn't mean you are out of the will of God. In fact, quite the opposite. God's will often involves very uncomfortable circumstances. Because of all that has happened with John and his family, my three children have learned that when the unthinkable happens, God is still in control. They saw that as you pray your way through a tragedy step-by-step, God brings good out of the situation. They know that when you walk closely with God and live in obedience to His ways, you can trust that you are in the center of His will, no matter what the circumstances are around you.

This experience and others have made me realize that the center of God's will is not a destination; it's the process itself. God's will is a place we choose to live every day as we seek intimate relationship with the Lord, lay a solid foundation in Him, and learn to walk in His way. As a young person, you have a lifetime ahead of you. Allow the Lord to bless you each day by walking with Him.

Prayer

Lord, help me always live in Your way so that I may continually find comfort in the center of Your will.

NOTES

CHAPTER 2

1. Rebecca St. James, *You're the Voice: 40 More Days with God* (Nashville: Thomas Nelson, 1997), 4.

CHAPTER 3

1. Misty Bernall, *She Said Yes* (Framington, Pa.: Plough Publishing House, 1999), 38–40.
2. Ibid., 81–82.
3. Ibid., 93.
4. Ibid., 12.
5. Beth Nimmo and Darrell Scott, *Rachel's Tears* (Nashville: Thomas Nelson, 2000), 27.
6. Ibid., 23
7. Ibid., 30.
8. Ibid., 97.

CHAPTER 5

1. Joanne Marxhausen, *Three in One* (St. Louis, Mo.: Concordia, 1973), 67.

CHAPTER 7

1. Jodi Berndt, *Celebration of Miracles* (Nashville: Thomas Nelson, 1995), 6–7.
2. Ibid., 10.

CHAPTER 8

1. Nimmo and Scott, *Rachel's Tears*, 29.

CHAPTER 9

1. Rebecca St. James, *You're the Voice: 40 More Days with God* (Nashville: Thomas Nelson, 1997), 23.
2. I have used the New Living Translation for these verses.

CHAPTER 11

1. Nimmo and Scott, *Rachel's Tears*, 47.

CHAPTER 12

1. Nimmo and Scott, *Rachel's Tears*, 42.

CHAPTER 13

1. Nimmo and Scott, *Rachel's Tears*, 171–172.

CHAPTER 16

1. Kevin Max, *Unfinished Work* (Nashville: Thomas Nelson, 2001), 84.
2. Nimmo and Scott, *Rachel's Tears*, 49.
3. Rebecca St. James, *Wait for Me* (Nashville: Thomas Nelson, 2002), 42–43.
4. Ibid., 49.

CHAPTER 17

1. St. James, *You're the Voice*, 58.

ABOUT THE AUTHOR

STORMIE OMARTIAN is a popular writer, accomplished lyricist, and speaker. She is the best-selling author of ten books, including *Praying God's Will for Your Life Workbook and Journal, The Power of a Praying Wife, The Power of a Praying Woman, Lord, I Want to Be Whole,* and *Stormie,* the story of her journey from the brokenness of being an abused child to becoming a whole person.

A popular media guest, Stormie has appeared on numerous radio and television programs, including *The 700 Club, Parent Talk, Homelife, Crosstalk,* and *Today's Issues.* Stormie speaks all over the United States in churches, women's retreats, and conferences. For twenty years Stormie has been encouraging women to pray for their families. She desires to help others become all that God created them to be, to establish strong family bonds and marriages, and to be instruments of God's love.

Stormie has been married to Grammy-winning record producer Michael Omartian for thirty years. They have three grown children, Christopher, Amanda, and John David.

You can contact Stormie through her Web site:

www.stormieomartian.com

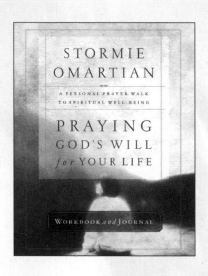

PRAYING GOD'S WILL FOR YOUR LIFE
WORKBOOK AND JOURNAL

AS YOU PRAY GOD'S WORD, YOU WILL SEE DYNAMIC growth take place in your life—you will become the person God intended you to be. Whether you are praying for specific needs— confidence, strength, patience, security, encouragement—or simply for a spiritual life, you will find the perfect prayers inside. With hundreds of prayers grouped according to topic and based entirely on Scripture, you will always have within your reach a rich source of personal, inspirational prayers.

0-7852-6407-8 | Trade Paper | 256 pages | $17.99